GLAMOUR
cakes

GLAMOUR

cakes

Eric Lanlard

foreword by Albert Roux

hamlyn

An Hachette Livre UK Company

First published in Great Britain in 2008 by
Hamlyn, a division of Octopus Publishing Group Ltd
2–4 Heron Quays, London E14 4JP
www.octopusbooks.co.uk

Copyright © Octopus Publishing Group Ltd 2008

Distributed in the United States and Canada by
Sterling Publishing Co., Inc.
387 Park Avenue South, New York, NY 10016-8810

Eric Lanlard asserts the moral right to be identified as the
author of this work

ISBN 978-0-600-61714-3

A CIP catalogue record for this book is available from the
British Library

Printed and bound in China

10 9 8 7 6 5 4 3 2 1

Note
Both metric and imperial measurements are given for the
recipes. Use one set of measures only, not a mixture of both.

Ovens should be preheated to the specified temperature.
If using a fan-assisted oven, follow the manufacturer's
instructions for adjusting the time and temperature.

This book includes dishes made with nuts and nut derivatives.
It is advisable for those with known allergic reactions to nuts and
nut derivatives and those who may be potentially vulnerable to
these allergies, such as pregnant and nursing mothers, invalids,
the elderly, babies and children, to avoid dishes made with nuts
and nut oils. It is also prudent to check the labels of preprepared
ingredients for the possible inclusion of nut derivatives.

It is advised that eggs should not be consumed raw. This book
contains some dishes made with raw or lightly cooked eggs.
It is prudent for more vulnerable people, such as pregnant and
nursing mothers, invalids, the elderly, babies and young children,
to avoid uncooked or lightly cooked dishes made with eggs.

Contents

Foreword

Over the 42 years of my professional life, literally thousands of young ladies and men have gone through my doors. Very few have marked me as much as this young man – Eric Lanlard. Furthermore, he became not just an employee, but a trusted member of the team. Although he left us many years ago, he has remained a dear friend of our family and we really cherish and rejoice in his success.

When I first met him he did not have to tell me he came from Brittany where he was born in Quimper in 1968 – he certainly has that Celtic look about him, as well as those fierce eyes full of determination to succeed. He settled into the job extremely quickly and commanded respect and admiration for his hard work from the people who worked under him.

Not only is he an artist in the decoration of cakes, but he also has a lot of imagination in finding new recipes for cakes and petit gateaux.

As far as we are concerned in our family, he deserves every success with his first book and we wish him well.

Albert H. Roux OBE

Introduction

I decided that I wanted to be *pâtissier* when I was very young. It wasn't a passing fad. Unlike my friends, who one day wanted to be firemen and the next astronauts, I was certain that I knew what I was going to do, and when I was 18 years old I became an apprentice at the *pâtisserie* Le Grand in Quimper in southern Brittany.

I had first decided that Le Grand was where I wanted to work when I was ten years old, and I spent eight long years drooling over the window displays in anticipation of the day I could begin what I regarded as my vocation. In the meantime, my parents and my family had to suffer years of experiments in our kitchen at home. Of course, I didn't choose to try the simplest recipes. Instead, I would embark on the most difficult creations, following the recipes a professional recipe book I had bought second-hand. I didn't have the right utensils or the right ingredients, and the results were more often disasters than successes. I quickly learned that you have to be both patient and well prepared before you start to make any desserts or cakes.

My two-year apprenticeship confirmed what I had known all along: this was my destiny. I was already planning where I wanted to go and how my own *pâtisserie* would look. However, as well as being thoroughly enjoyable, my apprenticeship was very hard work. From that September day when I walked into the small *laboratoire* at Le Grand I put my social life on hold for the rest of my life. I was fresh from college, and the early starts and having to work seven days a week and on every bank holiday, Christmas Day and New Year's Day came as something as a shock to my system, but it was all worthwhile. When I left I had a degree of experience and knowledge that I would never have expected to have achieved in such a short time. But I was still ready to learn more and more.

I have been extremely fortunate to work under some marvellous people, who have taken me under their wings and have shared with me their talents and their passions. Seeing their successes fuelled my own ambitions, but without their encouragement I don't think I would ever have dreamed about opening my own business – and definitely not one in a foreign country.

Over the last eleven years our little business has gone from strength to strength, and we regularly reinvent ourselves. The most important change was to set up Savoir Design, our bespoke celebration cake branch, which at last made it possible for me to talk to clients face to face and to make their dreams come true. Savoir Design allowed me to meet a wide range of people, from the unknown to some famous actors and models. No matter who they are, ultimately they come to us for one reason only: to celebrate an important occasion or date with something very special. And that's what we do, and we enjoy making people smile or even bringing tears to their eyes when they see their special cake.

Now I am starting a new venture. At last the glamorous *pâtisserie* I always dreamed about is opening, and, like my masters at Le Grand, Jean-Claude Arens and Albert Roux, I will be able to share my knowledge in our cookery school. I hope that with this, my first book, I will be able to give you a taste of my passion and my favourite inspirational designs. Remember, pastry is like chemistry: follow the recipes and take your time.

The Basics

Specialist Supplies

If you make cakes regularly you will already have most, if not all, of the items of equipment you will need to make the basic cakes used in this book. Icing and decorating them, however, will require some less usual items, and you might find that you have to get these from a specialist cookery shop or search for them on the internet.

Basic equipment

In addition to a good quality electric whisk and beaters, you will need nonstick cake tins, both square and round, in a range of sizes. You will also need:

- A large plastic board on which you can roll out marzipan and icing
- A sturdy, smooth-sided rolling pin to roll out marzipan and icing
- A small rolling pin to roll out petal paste for cutting out flowers
- A rolling pin with a textured surface
- A cake smoother
- Large and small palette knives
- Piping bags and greaseproof paper to make small bags for royal icing
- A range of nozzles for icing
- Pastry brushes
- Soft paintbrushes

Extra equipment

The cakes rest on cake drums (boards), which are widely available in a range of sizes and shapes from good cookery shops, although you might have to order some of the larger and smaller sizes specially. These are usually edged with satin ribbon, which is available in a range of widths and colours. You will need 15 mm (¾ inch) wide ribbon to edge most of the cake drums in this book, and the ribbon can be fastened in place with edible glue or a gluestick. Measure the length around the edge of the cake drum (board) before cutting the ribbon. You will also need a pair of sharp scissors and a plastic ruler to make sure that all edges are level and crisp. Among the other items that you will use are:

- Icing smoothers
- Plastic dowel rods, which are available in 20 cm (8 inch) and 30 cm (12 inch) lengths
- Cake pillars
- Cake cards (or cut your own from thin white card)
- Polystyrene cake dummies in various shapes, including cones
- Edible glue (available in liquid form) or a gluestick
- Tracing paper

- Ornamental flowers
- Flower, petal and leaf cutters
- A range of shaped cutters, including fans
- Marzipan fruit moulds
- Cherub mould
- Foam pad (sugarcraft flower pad)
- A grooved board on which to roll out petal paste to make leaves
- Scribing needle
- Quilting tool (stitch marker)
- Bone shaping/modelling tool
- Ball shaping/modelling tool

Edible decorations

Petal paste, which is also known as sugar florists' paste or flower paste, is available in a range of colours and is used to make flowers and other delicate decorations. It can be rolled out very thinly, so it is lightweight, and dries hard, with a porcelain-like finish. When you are using it remember that it dries very quickly, so cover unused petal paste with clingfilm or it will become unusable.

Ready-made modelling chocolate is available in 150 g (5 oz) and 1 kg (2 lb) packs, or you can make your own (see page 29).

You can buy 600 g (1 lb 3 oz) boxes, which contain 160 curls of milk and dark Belgian chocolate and you can buy an assortment of sizes of ready-made white, dark and milk chocolate roses. Chocolate cigarillos of the type used in Red Berry Romance (see pages 102–5) are available in 700 g (about 1½ lb) boxes, which hold 120 pieces.

If you run out of time or don't feel very artistic most sugarcraft shops and some shops that sell cooking equipment also sell ready-made cake decorations, including edible flowers, ladybirds and butterflies. Edible silver, gold and coloured balls (dragees) are always useful and are widely available.

You will also need a range of edible food dyes, both liquid and powder, and some food colouring pens, which are available in large cookery shops; alternatively, look on the internet. Use colouring

powders, including super white powder, to create subtle, professional-looking shades. They can be used with both sugarpaste and royal icing. Some cakes are decorated with lustre and pearlized colours, which are available in small jars. If you use pearl powder to paint you can use it neat or mix it with a little clear alcohol before applying it with a fine paintbrush. Mixing it with alcohol will allow you to cover a larger area and will give a less concentrated finish. Otherwise, simply use the powder to highlight the edges of petals or butterfly wings.

Basic Recipes – Cakes

Different Cake Shapes

On the following pages, the cake recipes that include a chart give the ingredients and cooking times for different sizes of cakes made in round tins. These ingredients and cooking times can be adapted to make different shaped cakes, as follows.

Heart-shaped

You can use the chart quantities to make the same sized heart-shaped cakes, although 10 cm (4 inch) heart-shaped tins are not available, so you would need to make a cake in a round tin and cut it out from a template. Heart-shaped cakes take a little longer to cook, so cook them at the longer time given for each cake and add 15 minutes. Then check to see if a skewer inserted into the centre of the cake comes out clean – if it does the cake is done.

Square

If you are using the chart recipe for a square cake remember to use a smaller tin – that is, the ingredients for a 20 cm (8 inch) round tin mixture will make an 18 cm (7 inch) square cake; those for a 25 cm (10 inch) round cake mixture will make a 23 cm (9 inch) square cake, and so on.

Mini

If you want to make 6 cm (2½ inch) mini cakes, such as those used for Champagne Bubbles (see pages 62–5), the ingredients for the 20 cm (8 inch) round tin will make 10–12 cakes, which will take about 30 minutes to cook, although the exact cooking time will depend on the depth of the cake mixture in the tins.

Vanilla Cake, Lemon Cake and Chocolate Cake

These three cakes can be made from the same basic ingredients – butter, caster sugar, eggs, plain flour and baking powder – the flavour depending on the additions. The method is the same for all three flavours. The table below shows the ingredients and cooking times for four sizes of round tin.

Ingredients	10 cm (4 inch)	15 cm (6 inch)	20 cm (8 inch)	25 cm (10 inch)
unsalted butter, softened	85 g (3¼ oz)	175 g (6 oz)	300 g (10 oz)	500 g (1 lb)
caster sugar	85 g (3¼ oz)	175 g (6 oz)	300 g (10 oz)	500 g (1 lb)
eggs, beaten	1 large	3 medium	5 medium	8 medium
plain flour, sifted	150 g (5 oz)	250 g (8 oz)	350 g (12 oz)	500 g (1 lb)
baking powder, sifted	¼ teaspoon	1 teaspoon	1½ teaspoons	2½ teaspoons
Vanilla cake				
vanilla extract	½ teaspoon	1 teaspoon	2 teaspoons	1 tablespoon
milk	1 tablespoon	1–2 tablespoons	2–3 tablespoons	3 tablespoons
Lemon cake				
lemon rind, grated	½ lemon	1 lemon	1 lemon	1 lemon
lemon juice	1 tablespoon	1–2 tablespoons	3 tablespoons	4 tablespoons
Chocolate cake				
cocoa powder, sifted	25 g (1 oz)	25 g (1 oz)	40 g (1½ oz)	65 g (2½ oz)
milk	1 tablespoons	2 tablespoons	2–3 tablespoons	4 tablespoons
cooking time	45–60 minutes	1–1¼ hours	1¼–1½ hours	1½–1¾ hours

one Butter and line the cake tin. Cream together the butter and sugar until light and fluffy. Gradually add the eggs, beating well.

two Fold the flour and baking powder with the lemon rind and juice (or the vanilla extract and milk or the cocoa powder and milk) into the cake batter.

three Transfer the mixture to the prepared tin and bake in a preheated oven, 180°C (350°F), Gas Mark 4, for the time indicated above or until the cakes are golden brown and springy to touch. Leave to cool in the tin for about 5 minutes before turning on to a wire rack to finish cooling.

Fruit Cake

When you are making a fruit cake it is especially important to recognize that all ovens vary, so the cooking times given here are only a guide. The cake is cooked when a skewer inserted into the centre comes out clean.

Ingredients	15 cm (6 inch)	20 cm (8 inch)	25 cm (10 inch)
sultanas	250 g (8 oz)	350 g (12 oz)	600 g (1 lb 3 oz)
raisins	250 g (8 oz)	350 g (12 oz)	600 g (1 lb 3 oz)
brandy	75 ml (3 fl oz)	150 ml (¼ pint)	200 ml (7 fl oz)
unsalted butter, softened	175 g (6 oz)	350 g (12 oz)	450 g (14½ oz)
dark soft brown sugar	150 g (5 oz)	300 g (10 oz)	400 g (13 oz)
eggs	2 large	4 large	6 large
plain flour, sifted	200 g (7 oz)	300 g (10 oz)	500 g (1 lb)
ground mixed spice	1 teaspoon	2 teaspoons	3 teaspoons
ground cinnamon	½ teaspoon	1 teaspoon	2 teaspoons
chopped mixed peel	60 g (2¼ oz)	150 g (5 oz)	175 g (6 oz)
glacé cherries, halved	50 g (2 oz)	100 g (3½ oz)	175 g (6 oz)
walnut halves	25 g (1 oz)	50 g (2 oz)	150 g (5 oz)
roasted hazelnuts	25 g (oz)	50 g (2 oz)	150 g (5 oz)
grated rind and juice	1–2 lemons	3 lemons	4 lemons
brandy, to soak	2 tablespoons	4 tablespoons	6 tablespoons
cooking time	2¼–3 hours	2½–3 hours	3½–4½ hours

one Soak the sultanas and raisins in the brandy overnight. Butter and line the sides and base of the cake tin.

two Drain the fruit, reserving the brandy. Cream together the butter and sugar until pale and light. Gradually beat in the eggs. Fold in the sifted flour and spices followed by the reserved brandy.

three Add the fruits, nuts, grated lemon rind and juice and fold together gently.

four Pour the mixture into the prepared tin and level the surface. Cover the top with a disc of greaseproof paper and cook in a preheated oven, 150°C (300°F), Gas Mark 2, for the times indicated above or until a skewer inserted into the centre comes out clean.

five Leave the cake to cool a little in the tin, turn it out on to a wire rack and add half of the brandy while it is still warm. When it is cold, add more brandy, wrap the cake in clingfilm and store in a cool, dry place until you are ready to decorate it. Stored correctly, the cake should keep for up to 6 months.

Carrot Cake

The ingredients listed here will make round cakes of the dimensions shown. Use deep tins, rather than the shallow ones you would use for a basic sponge. Instead of peanut (groundnut) oil you can use sunflower oil if you prefer.

Ingredients	15 cm (6 inch)	20 cm (8 inch)	25 cm (10 inch)
eggs	3 medium	5 medium	7 medium
soft light brown sugar	200 g (7 oz)	350 g (12 oz)	500 g (1 lb)
groundnut oil	250 ml (8 fl oz)	400 ml (14 fl oz)	500 ml (17 fl oz)
self-raising flour	200 g (7 oz)	400 g (13 oz)	550 g (1 lb 2 oz)
cinnamon	1 teaspoon	2 teaspoons	3 teaspoons
ground nutmeg	1 teaspoon	2 teaspoons	3 teaspoons
salt	pinch	pinch	pinch
carrots, peeled and finely grated	250 g (8 oz)	400 g (13 oz)	550 g (1 lb 2 oz)
sultanas	100 g (3½ oz)	200 g (7 oz)	300 g (12 oz)
chopped mixed nuts	100 g (3½ oz)	200 g (7 oz)	300 g (12 oz)
cooking time	1½–1¾ hours	2½–2¾ hours	3–3¼ hours

one Butter and line a cake tin. Beat together the eggs, sugar and oil for about 5 minutes.

two In a separate bowl mix together the flour, cinnamon, nutmeg and salt. Add the carrots, sultanas and nuts and fold into the egg mixture.

three Pour the mixture into the prepared tin and cook in a preheated oven, 150°C (300°F), Gas Mark 2, for the time indicated above until the cake is well risen and firm to touch. Leave the cake to cool before removing from the tin.

Chocolate Marquise

Keep this rich chocolate cake for special occasions. Use the best quality chocolate you can find and make sure it contains at least 70 per cent cocoa solids. Decorate the cake with fresh fruit that is in season. The ingredients listed here are sufficient to make one 20 cm (8 inch) round cake. If you use this cake as the basis of the Cherry Envelope (see pages 44–9) replace the cocoa powder with flour, use white chocolate in the glaze and mascarpone cream (see page 27) instead of chocolate mousse. You should also replace the chocolate ganache glaze with white chocolate ganache (see page 28).

Ingredients

250 g (8 oz) ground almonds

150 g (5 oz) caster sugar, plus 3 tablespoons

3 tablespoons cocoa powder, sifted

6 egg whites

375 g (12 oz) fresh raspberries

Chocolate mousse

250 g (8 oz) plain, dark chocolate, finely chopped

250 ml (8 fl oz) double cream

100 g (3½ oz) unsalted butter, softened and cut into cubes

Syrup

100 g (3½ oz) caster sugar

50 ml (2 fl oz) framboise (raspberry liqueur)

Chocolate ganache glaze

250 g (8 oz) plain, dark chocolate, chopped

250 ml (8 fl oz) milk

50 ml (2 fl oz) glucose syrup

50 g (2 oz) unsalted butter, softened and cut into cubes

one Butter and line a loose-bottomed 20 cm (8 inch) round cake tin. In a large bowl combine the almonds, 150 g (5 oz) caster sugar and cocoa powder.

two In a separate bowl beat the egg whites until stiff, add 3 tablespoons caster sugar and beat for 1 minute. Use a spatula to fold the egg white mixture gently into the almond mixture.

three Spoon the mixture into the prepared tin and bake in a preheated oven, 180°C (350°F), Gas Mark 4, for 25–35 minutes or until a metal skewer comes out clean. Leave to cool on a wire rack, then wrap in clingfilm.

four Meanwhile, prepare the chocolate mousse. Put the chocolate in a heatproof bowl. Put the cream in a saucepan, bring to the boil, pour over the chocolate and leave for a few minutes, then gently mix together. Stir in the butter. If the mixture starts to separate, put the bowl over a pan of simmering water and beat until smooth. Cover with clingfilm and leave at room temperature for 12 hours.

five Next day make the syrup by putting the caster sugar and 50 ml (2 fl oz) water in a pan. Bring to the boil, boil for 2 minutes, then leave to cool. When the syrup is cold, stir in the liqueur.

six Use an electric mixer to beat the chocolate mousse for 5 minutes. Cut the cake into three horizontal layers. (This isn't easy because the layers will be quite thin, so be careful.) Put one layer in a 20 cm (8 inch) cake tin and drizzle over 3–4 tablespoons syrup. Spread a layer of mousse on top, add another layer of sponge, drizzle with syrup and cover with more mousse. Cover the mousse with fresh raspberries, reserving 8–10 fruits, add the rest of the mousse and top with the final layer of sponge and a little more syrup. Chill for 4 hours.

seven Make the ganache by putting the chocolate in a heatproof bowl. Put the milk and glucose in a saucepan and bring to the boil. Pour the hot mixture over the chocolate and leave for 2 minutes, then stir gently and add the butter (take care not to over-beat the mixture). Chill for 25 minutes or until the mixture is the consistency of thick double cream.

eight When you are ready to serve the cake, use a cook's blowtorch or run a hot cloth around the outside of the cake tin to soften the chocolate so you can carefully remove it.

nine If you are serving this cake as it is and not as the basis for one of the other recipes, place the cake on a wire rack, pour over the ganache and smooth with a palette knife. Decorate it with white Belgian chocolate curls (see page 13) and a selection of fresh fruit, such as kiwifruit, peaches, strawberries, redcurrants and grapes, and the reserved raspberries.

Choux Pastry

Choux pastry is used to make profiteroles and is also used to make the buns used for Croquembouche (see pages 124–9). It can help to sift the flour, sugar and salt on to a piece of greaseproof paper so that you can slide it all into the liquid at one go. The ingredients below will make about 45 buns. If you are making a Croquembouche you will need 35 buns for each small cone, but always make a few extra in case some are misshapen.

Ingredients

105 g (3¾ oz) plain flour

pinch of salt

1 teaspoon caster sugar

75 g (3 oz) unsalted butter

200 ml (7 fl oz) water

3 medium eggs

one Line three baking sheets with baking parchment. Sift the flour with the salt and sugar. Repeat the sifting once more.

two Put the butter in a medium-sized pan with the water and heat gently until the butter has melted, then bring to the boil. Tip in the flour, all at once, and beat vigorously with a wooden spoon over a low heat until the dough leaves the sides of the pan and looks smooth. Cook over a low heat for a minute, stirring.

three Leave the mixture to cool for 3–4 minutes, then gradually mix in the eggs, whisking well after each addition. (You might find you do not need to add all the egg: the finished paste should hold its own shape and be stiff enough to pipe.)

four Use a piping bag and a small, plain tube to pipe small profiteroles on to the lined baking sheet. Bake in a preheated oven, 200°C (400°F), Gas Mark 6, for 20–25 minutes or until crisp. Remove the buns from the oven, leaving the oven on, and make a small hole on each side of each profiterole to let out the steam, then return them to the oven for a couple of minutes to make them crisp.

Macaroons

These ingredients are enough to make 60 macaroons, which are used in the Marie Antoinette Macaroon Tower on pages 72–5. For best results, always bake meringues slowly and at a low temperature and always use dried egg white, which is a concentrate. You'll find it in supermarkets with the other baking ingredients.

Ingredients

500 g (1 lb) icing sugar

250 g (8 oz) ground almonds

8 egg whites

40 g (1½ oz) dried egg white

50 g (2 oz) caster sugar

Flavouring

a few drops vanilla or raspberry extract *or* 20 g (¾ oz) cocoa powder *or* 20 g (¾ oz) pistachio paste

one Sift the icing sugar into a bowl with the ground almonds.

two In a separate bowl beat together the egg whites and dried egg white until half-risen. Add the caster sugar and beat until stiff peaks form.

three Stir either vanilla or raspberry extract into the egg white peaks. To make chocolate macaroons, sift the cocoa into the almond mixture and beat until firm. For almond-flavoured macaroons, sprinkle the pistachio paste on to the egg whites. Gently fold the flavouring in with a spatula or metal spoon, but be careful not to overmix or the mixture will turn to liquid.

four Line a baking sheet with greaseproof paper and add a little of the mixture to each corner to secure the paper. With a piping bag fitted with a 1.5–2 mm (¹⁄₁₆–¹⁄₁₈ inch) round nozzle pipe small mounds, about 2.5 cm (1 inch) across, on to the paper. Make sure they are not too close together because they will expand during cooking. Leave the macaroons for 10–12 minutes to *croûte* (form a light crust on the outside) then bake them in a preheated oven, 180°C (350°F), Gas Mark 4, for about 10 minutes or until hard.

five To help separate the macaroons lift the paper slightly and run a little cold water between the paper and the baking sheet. After 2–3 minutes the two should separate easily. Leave the macaroons to cool on the tray then sandwich them together with 200 g (7 oz) Chocolate Ganache or Vanilla Buttercream (see pages 24 and 28), or raspberry jam.

Basic Recipes – Icings & Fillings

Ready-made icings and fillings

On the following pages, you will find recipes for a variety of icings and fillings but many of these can be bought ready-made from specialist cake decorating suppliers or in powder form to mix at your convenience. There is usually a variety of flavours, colours and quantities available.

Sugarpaste and petal paste

Sugarpaste is a fondant-like icing that can be used both to cover cakes and cake drums and to make small decorations. Petal paste is an icing used to make sugar flowers and decorations. It can be rolled out much thinner than other icings and dries hard. There is no recipe here for homemade sugarpaste or petal paste as they are so widely available in a great variety of colours that it is much easier to buy them ready-made.

Sugarpaste is available in ready-to-roll packs of 500 g (1 lb). Always make sure you have enough to cover your cake or cakes before you begin, especially if you are doing the colouring yourself – it is very difficult to get two batches of icing to match exactly in colour. See page 31 for a guide to quantities and remember to add extra to cover the drum.

Petal paste comes in packs of 125–500 g (4 oz–1 lb). It is also known as sugar florist paste and flower paste.

Always make sure you allow sufficient time for the sugarpaste or icing to set and for any decorations you make from petal paste to dry.

Royal Icing

These ingredients will give you about 500 g (1 lb) icing, which is sufficient to decorate any of the cakes in this book. Make sure you use salmonella-free egg whites. If you are worried about using raw eggs in your icing you can buy reconstituted albumen powder, which replaces the raw egg. Follow the instructions on the packet for making the icing. Throughout the book, nozzle sizes are given for use with a piping bag. If you prefer, you can make your own icing cone out of greaseproof paper and snip off the end.

Ingredients

2 medium egg whites
1 teaspoon lemon juice
about 500 g (1 lb) icing sugar, sieved

one Tip the egg whites into a bowl and stir in the lemon juice. Gradually add the sieved icing sugar, mixing well after each addition.

two Continue adding small amounts of icing sugar until you achieve the desired consistency. For piping the icing should be fairly stiff but not too stiff to pipe.

Colouring royal icing

Transfer the amount of icing you need to a small bowl. Because edible food colouring paste is highly concentrated, you will need only a tiny amount of colour, so dip a cocktail stick into the colouring paste and mix the icing thoroughly before you add any more colouring paste or you could end up with streaks in the icing.

Buttercream

The ingredients here will make about 3.5 kg (7¾ lb), which is sufficient to fill and cover a three-tier cake consisting of 15 cm (6 inch), 20 cm (8 inch) and 25 cm (10 inch) cakes.

Ingredients

500 g (1 lb) granulated sugar
150 ml (¼ pint) water
25 g (1 oz) glucose syrup
2 vanilla pods
300 g (10 oz) egg yolks (about 15)
1 kg (2 lb) unsalted butter, softened

one Tip the sugar, water and glucose syrup into a heavy-based saucepan and bring slowly to the boil. When the sugar has dissolved, boil until the mixture reaches 124°C (255°F).

two Remove the seeds from the vanilla pod and add them to a bowl with the egg yolks. Very gradually whisk in the sugar mixture. Discard the vanilla pods.

three When the mixture is cold, gradually whisk in the softened butter until light and fluffy.

Variations

Lemon buttercream

After adding the butter, add 1 tablespoon of lemon juice and enough grated lemon rind to give a good flavour. Add extra icing sugar to thicken or extra lemon juice to make it runnier, as necessary.

Chocolate buttercream

After adding the butter, add 350 g (11½ oz) melted dark chocolate.

Crème Pâtissière

This will make sufficient filling, about 750 g (1½ lb), for about 45 choux buns (see page 20). The filling for the choux buns in Croquembouche (see pages 124–9) is flavoured with the finely grated rind of half an orange.

Ingredients

500 ml (17 fl oz) milk

100 g (3½ oz) caster sugar

1 vanilla pod, split lengthways

4 large egg yolks

50 g (2 oz) cornflour

25 g (1 oz) chilled unsalted butter

one Put the milk in a heavy-based saucepan and add 20 g (¾ oz) sugar and the vanilla pod and bring to the boil.

two Beat together the egg yolks and the remaining sugar, add the cornflour and a little milk to thin, and stir well. Add to the milk and sugar mixture and bring to the boil again, stirring constantly until the mixture is smooth and very thick.

three Remove the saucepan from the heat, remove and discard the vanilla pod, beat in the butter and leave to cool.

Mascarpone Cream

Use this delicious cream to fill the cakes used in the Cherry Envelope (see pages 44–7). These ingredients will make about 800 g (1 lb 10 oz), which is sufficient for filling and covering one 20 cm (8 inch) cake.

Ingredients

250 g (8 oz) mascarpone
50 g (2 oz) vanilla sugar
500 ml (17 fl oz) double cream

one Beat together the mascarpone and sugar until the mixture is smooth.

two Fold the double cream into the mixture and whip until a soft peak is reached.

Caramel

Caramel is used for spun sugar in the Croquembouche (see pages 124–9). You will need to make it in two batches so that it doesn't burn. If the caramel becomes too thick when you are using it, return the pan to a very gentle heat and stir it occasionally.

Ingredients

175 g (6 oz) caster sugar
175 ml (6 fl oz) water

one Heat the sugar and water over a gentle heat. **Do not stir** or the sugar granules will crystallize on the sides of the saucepan.

two When the sugar has dissolved, boil until the mixture is rich brown.

three Dip the saucepan into a bowl of cold water as soon as the caramel is ready and leave it for 30 seconds. This will prevent it from cooking further.

Chocolate Ganache

You can buy ready-made chocolate ganache, but if you prefer to make your own these ingredients will make about 850 g (1 lb 11 oz) of icing, which will be enough to fill and cover the top and sides of a 20 cm (8 inch) cake. Use the best quality plain dark chocolate you can find and always check the cocoa content and make sure that the only fat it contains is cocoa butter. White chocolate ganache can be made by simply replacing the dark chocolate with white.

Ingredients

300 ml (10 fl oz) double cream

40 g (1½ oz) glucose syrup

450 g (14½ oz) good quality plain, dark chocolate, chopped

75 g (3 oz) unsalted butter, softened

one Put the cream and glucose syrup in a heavy-based saucepan and heat until just boiling.

two Pour the mixture over the chopped chocolate and mix gently until smooth. When it is lukewarm, gently mix in the softened butter.

three Leave the ganache to set at room temperature or in the refrigerator.

Modelling Chocolate

Ready-made modelling chocolate is widely available, in both dark and white chocolate versions, but it is possible to make your own, and the ingredients here will make about 2.5 kg (5 lb). The same method can be used with plain, dark chocolate. Make sugar syrup from equal quantities of water and caster sugar, here 150 ml (¼ pint) water and 150 g (5 oz) sugar have been used.

Ingredients

- 1.75 kg (3½ lb) good quality white chocolate, chopped
- 100 g (3½ oz) cocoa butter, chopped
- 375 ml (13 fl oz) glucose syrup
- 300 ml (½ pint) sugar syrup

Note

The mixture will go very grainy before becoming smooth again. When kneading and moulding, do not overwork the chocolate, as the cocoa butter will rise to the surface and 'bloom' as it heats. If this happens, return the chocolate to the refrigerator until it hardens again, then rework.

one Put the chocolate in a heatproof bowl suspended over a pan of simmering water and leave it to melt. Put the cocoa butter in a separate bowl and melt it in the same way.

two Put the glucose and sugar syrups in a heavy-based saucepan and heat but do not boil. Stir the syrup into the melted chocolate, add the melted cocoa butter and mix thoroughly with a wooden spoon for about 10 minutes.

three Transfer the mixture to a plastic bag, seal the bag and set aside for at least 12 hours before using. It will harden to a clay-like texture.

four When you are ready, knead the chocolate until it is smooth and pliable and use it to mould fans or roses, or to cover cakes.

Basic Techniques

Covering Cake Drums

It is a good idea to start by decorating the base on which your cake will sit. You can cover a cake drum with sugarpaste or with melted chocolate, depending on how you intend to decorate your cake. If you want the colour of the sugarpaste on the drum and the cake to match, remember to add extra to the amounts shown in the chart opposite, so it can all be coloured at the same time. The drum should always be at least 5 cm (2 inches) larger than the cake that sits directly on top of it, but can be bigger. Taller cakes will benefit from the support of two drums (the bottom one larger than the top one) but multiple boards can also be used for decorative purposes.

Covering a cake drum with sugarpaste

Roll out the sugarpaste so that it is just larger than the drum and carefully lift it over the drum. Trim the edge with a sharp knife, then cut out a hole the same size and shape as the base of the cake in the centre of the sugarpaste. With the cake in position, use your fingers to smooth the sugarpaste to the edge of the cake, then pipe a row of 'pearls' to disguise the join.

If you are covering two drums with sugarpaste, cover the lower drum first, cutting out the space for the top drum. If the drums are square, cut strips for the lower one, carefully mitring the joints at the corners so that they fit together snugly (see Peony Perfection page 106 for an example). Finish the top drum as described above. Use a little royal icing to stick the drums together.

Covering a cake drum with chocolate

Gently melt the chocolate in a heatproof bowl set above a saucepan of simmering water. Use a large, soft paintbrush to coat the drum in a thin layer of chocolate, working from edge to edge.

Covering Cakes

Most cakes in this book are covered with sugarpaste before being decorated. It forms a smooth base and can be made into almost any colour you can imagine. If you are using a fruit cake, it is traditional to first cover it with marzipan and then with sugarpaste.

Calculating quantities of marzipan and icing

The following table is a guide to the amounts of sugarpaste and marzipan needed to cover the top and sides of a range of cakes, either 8 cm (3 inches) or 10 cm (4 inches) deep. Add an extra 10 per cent of the quantity to allow for enough sugarpaste to cover each drum you are using.

Cake Size	Round/Heart 3-inch deep	Round/Heart 4-inch deep	Square 3-inch deep	Square 4-inch deep
10–15 cm (4–6 inches)	350 g (11½ oz)	420 g (13¾ oz)	500 g (1 lb)	600 g (1 lb 3½ oz)
18 cm (7 inches)	500 g (1 lb)	600 g (1 lb 3½ oz)	575 g (1 lb 2½ oz)	690 g (1 lb 6 oz)
20 cm (8 inches)	575 g (1 lb 2½ oz)	690 g (1 lb 6 oz)	800 g (1 lb 10 oz)	960 g (1 lb 14½ oz)
23 cm (9 inches)	800 g (1 lb 10 oz)	960 g (1 lb 14½ oz)	950 g (1 lb 14 ½ oz)	1.1 kg (2 lb 4 oz)
25 cm (10 inches)	950 g (1 lb 14½ oz)	1.1 kg (2 lb 4 oz)	1 kg (2 lb)	1.2 kg (2 lb 5 oz)
28 cm (11 inches)	1 kg (2 lb)	1.2 kg (2 lb 5 oz)	1.2 kg (2 lb 6 oz)	1.4 kg (2 lb 12½ oz)
30 cm (12 inches)	1.2 kg (2 lb 6 oz)	1.4 kg (2 lb 12½ oz)	1.3 kg (2 lb 10 oz)	1.6 kg (3 lb 3 oz)
33 cm (13 inches)	1.8 kg (3 lb 10 oz)	2.2 kg (4 lb 6 oz)	1.9 kg (3 lb 14 oz)	2.3 kg (4 lb 10 oz)
35 cm (14 inches)	1.9 kg (3 lb 14 oz lb)	2.3 kg (4 lb 10 oz)	2 kg (4 lb)	2.4 kg (4 lb 13 oz)

Covering a cake with marzipan

Fruit cakes are traditionally covered with marzipan before they are iced, but you could leave out this layer if you don't like marzipan. If necessary, cut the cake so that the top and bottom are flat.

one

one If you are covering a fruit cake, brush the cake with brandy then brush it with hot, sieved apricot jam. If you are covering a sponge cake, split and fill it with icing and jam, as liked, and cover it with a thin layer of buttercream or apricot glaze. Set the cake on a suitable cake drum or card.

two Knead the marzipan until it is soft, then roll it out on a work surface lightly dusted with icing sugar to a circle or square 5 cm (2 inches) larger than the top and sides of the cake. The marzipan should be about 5 mm (¼ inch) thick. Carefully lift the marzipan over the cake, then smooth over the top and down the sides. If you are covering a square cake take care to flare out the corners.

three Gently rub the marzipan in circular movements with the palms of your hands until smooth. Finish smoothing the surface with an icing smoother if you have one. Use a sharp knife to trim the excess marzipan from the base of the cake, cutting down on to the drum or plate so that the marzipan is flush with the drum. Leave the marzipan to dry for 12 hours or overnight.

two

three

Covering a cake with sugarpaste

If you are covering a marzipan-covered fruit cake, brush the surface of the marzipan with a little cooled boiled water so that the sugarpaste will stick to it. If you are covering a sponge cake, cut off any bumps to level the top. Split and fill it with icing and jam, as liked, and cover it with a thin layer of buttercream or apricot glaze. Set the cake on a suitable cake drum or card.

one

two

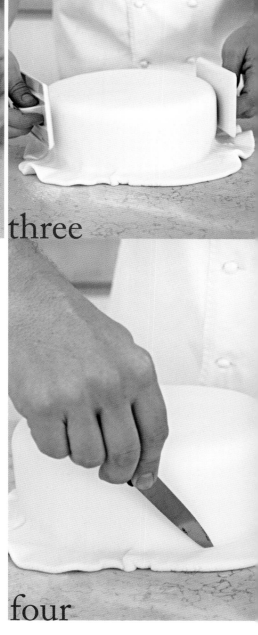

three

four

one
Brush the surface of the marzipan (if used) with a little cooled boiled water so that the sugarpaste will stick to it. If you are covering a sponge cake cut off any bumps to level the top. Knead the sugarpaste until soft, then roll it out on a work surface lightly dusted with icing sugar to a circle or square 5 cm (2 inches) larger than the top and sides of the cake. Carefully lift the sugarpaste over the cake, then smooth over the top and down the sides. Flare out the corners if the cake is square.

two
Using the side of your hand, tuck in the sugarpaste around the bottom of the cake.

three
Gently rub the surface of the cake with circular movements of your hands to give a smooth finish and, if liked, finish off with a special icing smoother.

four
Use a sharp knife to trim the excess icing from the base of the cake, cutting neatly down to the drum. Leave in a cool place for 24 hours to allow the icing to become firm.

Constructing a Tiered Cake

Many cakes – most of the cakes you make, in fact – are single-tier cakes. But there is nothing quite so dramatic as a two-, three- or even four-tiered cake. They really are glamorous and spectacular, which is why tiered cakes are so often chosen for weddings and other special celebrations. Once you have decided on the kind of cake you want, give a little thought to what you want the overall effect to be. How much space do you have? How easy is it going to be to assemble on the day? Remember, always have the lightest and smallest cake on the top.

Stacking a cake

You can stack cakes one on top of the other without using traditional cake pillars, but it is important that you use dowel rods to support each cake. If you do not, the cakes sitting immediately on top of each other will slowly but surely sink into each other. Each cake must be sitting on its own cake drum or piece of card, which must (except for the lowest tier) be the same diameter as the cake.

When you are stacking cakes, make sure each dowel rod is cut to about 2 mm (less than ⅛ inch) more than the depth of the cake. As you insert the dowel rod into the cake, mark a line on each dowel rod and then use strong scissors to trim it to the correct length. This arrangement supports the cake above, but the dowel rods will be hidden.

You can stack cakes separated by polystyrene central columns, but, again, the columns must be supported by hidden dowel rods (see Blocking a cake, page 36).

one

two

one Measure the position of the dowel rods: as a marker, use something the same shape ans size as the next tier, such as a cake card, bowl, plate or polystyrene block. Hold this on top of the larger tier and mark around the edge with a pin or dowel rod.

two Place the dowel rods into the cake just inside the marked perimeter (four for a square cake, three for a round cake, plus one extra in the centre). Use a knife to mark each one just above the top of the cake. Alternatively, measure them with a ruler.

three Take out the dowel rods and cut them to size. When replaced, they should be just visible.

four Smooth some royal icing over the centre of the cake, covering the top of the dowel rods. Rest the next tier, iced on to a drum, on top of the rods.

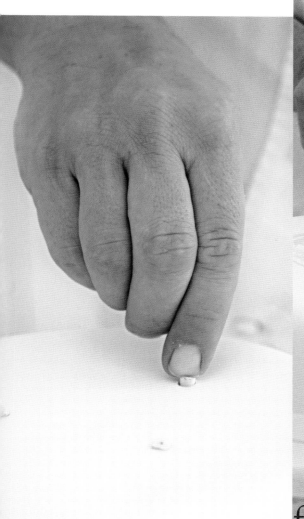

three

four

one

two

Blocking a cake

Many of the cakes in this book are mini cakes on iced stands, and I have used sugarpaste to cover the drum and then used a little royal icing to fasten a polystyrene block on a lower drum so that the block supports the upper drum. The mini cakes then obscure the polystyrene block, although the block can be decorated with ribbon. Alternatively, you can cover the drum and polystyrene block with melted chocolate.

If your design includes large cakes you will need to use dowel rods to help support the weight of the cake.

three

one Choose a polystyrene block just a little smaller than the circumference of the cake that will sit on top of it. Place it at the centre of the lower cake and push dowel rods through the polystyrene block and into the cake. Use a knife to mark each dowel rod 1–2 mm (less than ⅛ inch) above the top of the cake. Alternatively, measure them with a ruler.

two Remove the dowel rods and cut them to size. Replace them into the block and cake: they should be just visible above the top of the block. Smooth some royal icing over the centre of the block, covering the top of the dowel rods. Rest the next tier, sitting on a cake card, on top of the block.

three The cakes now sit on top of each other, separated by a polystyrene block which is narrower than both the cakes. This gap is best filled with fresh flowers. Follow the instructions for wiring flowers on page 40 and insert them into the polystyrene block. It is easier to insert flowers into the polystyrene block with the top tier removed.

Using pillars

If you prefer to use pillars to separate the cake tiers mark the position of the pillars as you do for dowel rods above.

one

two

three

one Insert dowel rods into the cake, drop a pillar over them and use a knife to mark each dowel rod 1–2 mm (about ⅛ inch) above the top of the pillar.

two Cut or snap the dowel rods to length, then reinsert them into the cake and replace the pillars. Rest the next tier, iced on to a cake board, on top of the pillars.

three The cakes can then be decorated with flowers or however you wish.

Finishing Touches

A lot of work goes into decorating any cake, but you have to make sure that you put as much effort into the minor details if you want to impress. The following pages will show you some simple techniques for adding the final touches of glamour to your cakes.

Ribbons and Bows

Finishing a cake drum with a ribbon not only makes a tidy edge but is elegant and simple to do. Hand tied bows will suit certain cakes but others will call for a neater flat bow.

Ribboning a drum

Ribbons are used to cover the edges of the cake drums, most of which are 15 mm (¾ inch) deep. Satin ribbon is available in a wide range of colours from most cookery shops.

one

two

three

one Measure the ribbon around the finished drum to make sure you have enough. Run edible glue or a gluestick around the edge of the drum.

two Run the ribbon around the drum, pressing firmly to secure it.

three Trim the end, leaving a short overlap, and use more glue to secure the end in place. The ribbon can also be cut it to length, with a short overlap, before gluing.

Making a neat bow

Conventionally tied bows suit certain cakes but can look a bit messy. These square, flat bows make a very elegant finish to any cake.

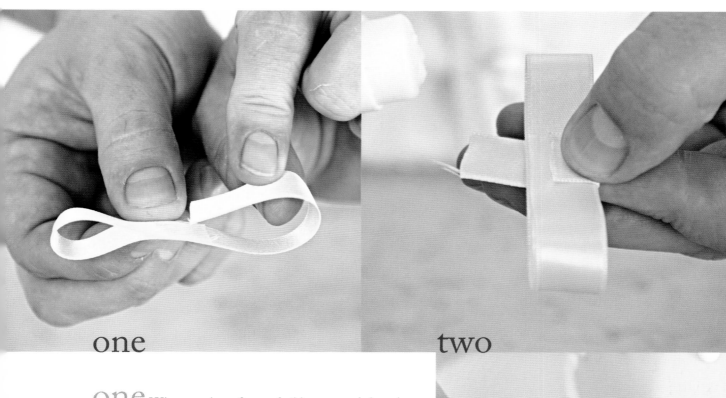

one

two

one When you have fastened ribbon around the cake or drum, make a bow by cutting a length of ribbon, putting a blob of glue in the centre and bending the ends into the centre, pressing down to secure them.

two Wrap a short length of ribbon vertically around the centre of the 'bow', overlapping the ends at the back and gluing them together. If you want, add tails by gluing individual lengths of ribbon.

three Glue the bow on to the ribboned drum.

To make a bow from sugarpaste or modelling chocolate, see 1950s Glamour Cake (pages 144–9).

three

Working with Fresh Flowers

Some of the most striking cakes are actually composed of very few elements.
A simple but effective result can be achieved by icing a cake with sugarpaste and
then embellishing it with fresh flowers. Make sure you buy flowers that are fresh
and in full bloom and choose those that keep well out of water (your florist should
be able to advise). Cut the stamens from lilies, as the pollen can stain the icing.

Wiring flowers

You will need 28 gauge florists' wire and green
florists' tape.

one Cut off the flowerhead, leaving a short
stem. Cut the wire in half and push one end into
the stem.

two Dampen the tape so that it sticks
to the wire, and wind it round the wire to about
halfway down. Insert the wired flowers into the
polystyrene block or into the cake.

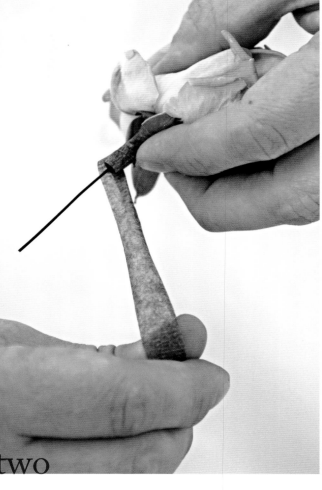

one

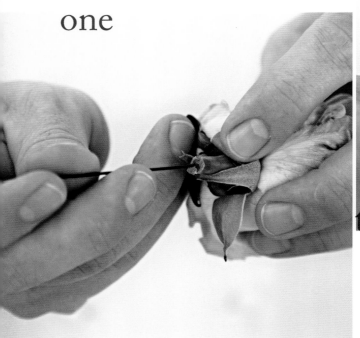

two

Crystallizing flowers and fruit

Some small flowers, such as violets, and other edible petals, such as roses, are often crystallized to add delicate and colourful decorations to cakes. Make sure the flowers and petals you choose are fresh, dry and unblemished. The same technique can be used to add a frosty look to certain fruits, particularly berries.

one

two

three

one Lightly beat together two egg whites in a small bowl. Have 200 g (7 oz) caster sugar in a separate bowl or dish.

two Immerse the flowers in the egg mixture and shake gently to remove the excess.

three Dip the flowers into the sugar. Transfer them to greaseproof paper to dry before using them on your cake. Fruit can also be crystallized in the same way.

The Cakes

Cherry Envelope

This modern-looking design is perfect for a summer celebration. If you prefer, you can make it as a single tier, and you could use other seasonal fruits instead of cherries. You can use any type of cake you wish – the smooth white chocolate that covers the cakes will be a good accompaniment for most fillings – but the cherries go particularly well with a white chocolate marquise (see page 16). You can freeze the marquise layers before stacking and decorating them, while still frozen, which makes them easier to move. The undecorated marquise will keep for up to a month in the freezer.

Ingredients

15 cm (6 inch) square cake, 10 cm (4 inches) deep

20 cm (8 inch) square cake, 10 cm (4 inches) deep

250 g (8 oz) white chocolate, melted

700 g (1 lb 6½ oz) white chocolate ganache (see page 28)

icing sugar, to dust

white modelling chocolate (see page 23)

fresh cherries

To assemble the cake

30 cm (12 inch) square cake drum

15 cm (6 inch) square cake card

5 dowel rods

large soft paintbrush

small palette knife

rolling pin

metal ruler

pastry brush

one

one Stack your chosen cakes together (see pages 34–5) and use a large, soft brush to paint the drum with melted white chocolate (see page 30).

two With a small palette knife, cover and smooth the outside of the cakes with the melted white chocolate ganache.

two

three

four

three Lightly dust your work surface with icing sugar and roll out the white modelling chocolate to make two strips, each 11.5 cm (4½ inches) deep, one 60 cm (24 inches) long and one 80 cm (32 inches) long, to cover the sides of the cakes. Use a ruler to trim the bottom and top edges to make sure they are perfectly level.

four Using a palette knife, carefully position the stacked cakes in the centre of the chocolate-painted drum.

five Lift the strips and apply them gently around the sides of each cake.

five

six Make sure that all the joints meet at the back of the cake. The top edges of both strips will stand about 1.5 cm (½ inch) above the tops of the cakes. Dip a brush in a little hot water and smooth the joints.

seven Roll out more white modelling chocolate and cut eight triangles, all 11.5 cm (4½ inches) deep for the corners. The ones for the upper tier should be 15 cm (6 inches) along the base; the ones for the lower tier should be 20 cm (8 inches) along the base. Secure the triangles to each corner with some melted white chocolate.

six

seven

eight Fill the gap between the tiers with fresh cherries, dipping the cherries in a little melted white chocolate to hold them in position. Pile cherries on top of the cake and place a few on the cake board.

Sweet Pea Spray

Sugar flowers went out of fashion some time ago, perhaps because we all got so used to seeing them. However, with a little patience almost any flower can be made, and these delicate sweet peas, which are made from petal paste, are a perfect example of a delightful craft.

Ingredients

20 cm (8 inch) round cake, 8 cm (3 inches) deep

632 g (1 lb 4 oz) white sugarpaste

200 g (7 oz) pale pink petal paste

green, violet- and fuchsia-coloured petal dust

100 g (3½ oz) light green petal paste

250 g (8 0z) white royal icing

pearl dust

clear alcohol

To assemble the cake

25 cm (10 inch) round cake drum

no. 22 light green florist's wire

craft pliers

small rolling pin

sweet pea petal cutters

no. 2 and no. 5 soft paintbrushes

foam pad

bone modelling tool

calyx cutter

light green florist's tape

grooved board

leaf cutter

crumpled foil

posy pick

piping bag and no. 3 nozzle

15 mm (¾ inch) wide lilac ribbon

edible glue

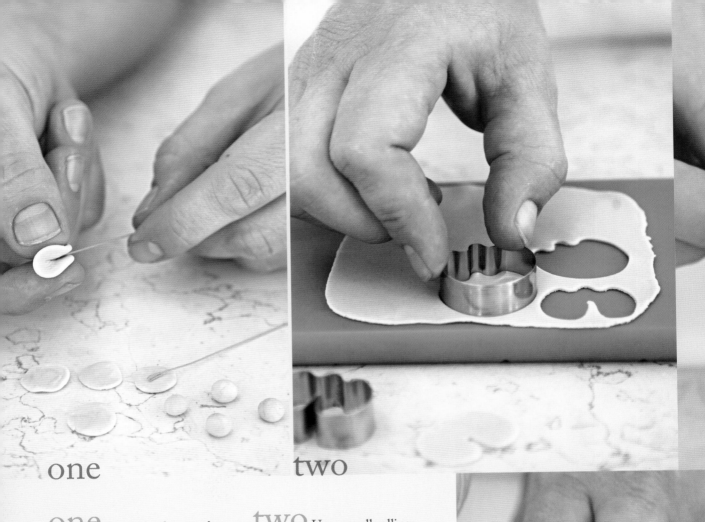

one

two

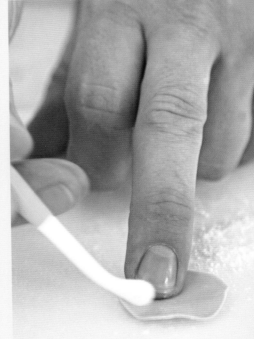

one Cover the drum and cake with sugarpaste (see pages 30–33). Cut the florist's wire into 15 cm (6 inch) lengths. Bend one end of each piece into a hook. Roll out a small ball of pink petal paste and flatten it with your fingers. Wrap this round the hooked end of a length of florist's wire to make the first petal.

two Use a small rolling pin to roll out some pink petal paste until it is fairly thin. Use the cutters to cut out the petals.

three Flute the smaller petal on a foam pad, using a bone modelling tool.

three

four

four Wrap the second petal around the small, wired petal and pinch them together at the base. Prop the flower against a piece of foam so that the petals do not get bent or crushed as they dry.

five Repeat the process with the medium-sized petal, fluting it round the top edge and pinching it on to the back of the flower. If the petals will not stick in place, brush on a tiny amount of hot water. Leave the flower to dry.

five

six Make the large petal in the same way, and attach it to the flower so that the round edge is at the top of the flower. Leave to dry.

seven Mix together some violet and fuchsia petal dust and use a no. 5 brush to highlight the flowers.

six

eight

eight Roll out some light green petal paste and use a calyx cutter to cut 12 calyces. Brush the bottom of each flower with a little hot water, thread a wire though the centre of a calyx and push it up to the base of the flower.

nine

nine Bind the wire with light green florist's tape, starting at the free end and working up to the flower. Make sure the wire is completely covered and dampen the tape to hold the end in place.

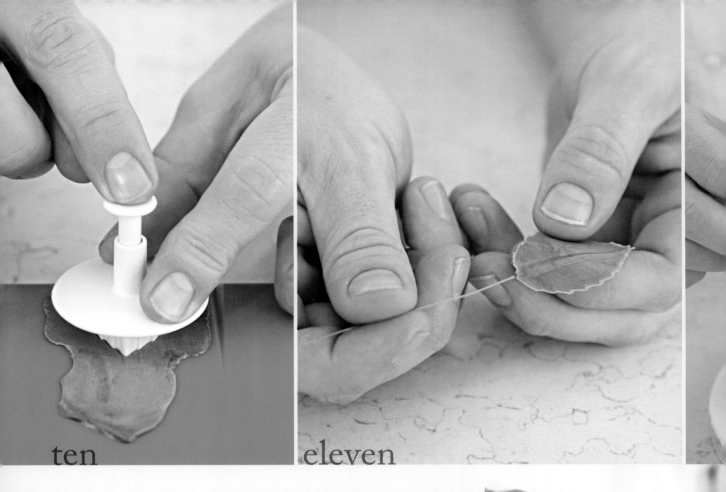

ten

eleven

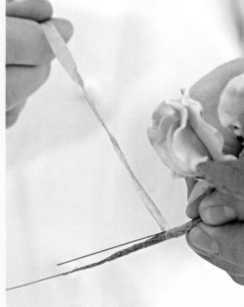

ten Make the leaves by rolling out green petal paste on the grooved board. Use a leaf cutter to cut a leaf.

eleven Eject the leaf from the cutter and carefully lay a 15 cm (6 inch) length of florist's wire along the ridge on the back of the leaf. Pinch the ends of the leaf to curve them slightly. Leave the leaves to dry for about 1 hour. You can place the soft leaves on crumpled foil to dry to make them look natural. They can be highlighted with a different shade of green dust.

twelve Attach a wired leaf to two wired flowers with florist's tape. Repeat this three times to create three sprays of two flowers and one leaf or, if you prefer, make sprays of different numbers of flowers and leaves.

twelve

Variation Cutters are available for a wide variety of petal and leaf types so you can let your imagination run wild. Try fashioning these deep red roses in petal paste, building them up in the same way as the white modelling chocolate roses on pages 138–43. They look stunning with lily of the valley and the wires mean the flowers and leaves look as if they are rustling and swaying in a breeze.

thirteen

thirteen Push a posy pick into the centre of the cake, bend the end of each of the sprays and insert them into the posy pick. Finish off the cake by using a no. 3 nozzle and white royal icing to pipe a row of 'pearls' around the bottom of the cake. Leave the icing to dry for about 2 hours and then use a no. 2 brush to paint them with pearl dust mixed with clear alcohol. Secure the ribbon around the edge of the drum and glue the ends in place.

Rococo
Extravaganza

This centrepiece will be the talking point of your party, and it proves that a wedding cake doesn't have to be white. Bold colours and a striking design will make your cake stand out in the room. This cake can be made using any colour sugarpaste and metallic dust to fit the theme of your event.

Ingredients

2 x 10 cm (4 inch) round cakes, 10 cm (4 inches) deep

2 x 15 cm (6 inch) round cakes, 10 cm (4 inches) deep

1.5 kg (3 lb) sugarpaste

purple edible dye

500g (1 lb) silver royal icing

grey edible dye

200 g (7 oz) petal paste

light silver metallic dust powder

clear alcohol

To assemble the cake

20 cm (8 inch) diameter cake drum

25 cm (10 inch) diameter cake drum

10 cm (4 inch) round cake card

4 dowel rods

piping bag and no. 2 and no. 3 nozzles

no. 1 paintbrush

florists' pins

15 mm (¾ inch) wide silver ribbon

edible glue or a gluestick

one

two

One Trim the cakes and use buttercream to stick them together in pairs to make two tiers, each 10 cm (4 inches) deep. Colour the sugar paste the right shade of purple. Cover the drums and two tiers with sugarpaste and stack them together (see pages 30–35). Use a no. 3 nozzle to pipe a row of small 'pearls' around the base of each cake, using some light grey royal icing.

two Use a no. 2 nozzle to pipe the C shapes and teardrops. Leave to dry for about 1 hour.

three Colour some petal paste light grey and roll out a thin tube with your fingers. Pinch it into pieces 24 cm (9½ inches) long with your fingers and smooth into points at each end. Carefully curl them into scroll shapes with the centres touching. Leave them to dry.

three

four

five

six

four Use a no. 1 paintbrush to paint over the piped Cs and the 'pearls' with light silver metallic dust powder. Leave to dry.

five When the scrolls are dry, paint these with light silver metallic dust powder mixed with a little clear alcohol.

six Attach the scrolls to the cake with little pieces of purple royal icing and support them with florists' pins until they are set. (Don't forget to remove the pins when the icing has set.) Fasten ribbon around the drums and glue the ends together.

Champagne
Bubbles

These cute little cakes are perfect if you want to make something different. The pearlized bubbles bring to mind a glass of champagne and are so simple to pipe, yet so elegant. The final tier can be one large cake, as shown, or you could have mini cakes all the way to the top.

Ingredients

23 mini cakes, each 5 cm (2 inches) across

15 cm (6 inch) round cake, 8 cm (3 inches) deep

4.5 kg (9 lb) white sugarpaste

500 g (1 lb oz) white royal icing

pearl dust

clear alcohol

in-season flowers to decorate (we used alstroemerias)

To assemble the cake

23 x 6 cm (2½ inch) round cake cards

2 x 20 cm (8 inch) round cake drums

25 cm (10 inch) round cake drum

30 cm (12 inch) round cake drum

piping bag and nos 2 and 1.5 nozzles

no. 3 paintbrush

7 cm (3 inch) polystyrene block, 7 cm (3 inches) deep

10 cm (4 inch) polystyrene block, 7 cm (3 inches) deep

15 cm (6 inch) polystyrene block, 7 cm (3 inches) deep

15 mm (¾ inch) white ribbon

edible glue or a gluestick

one Place each of the mini cakes on a cake card. Cover all the cake drums and the cakes with white sugarpaste (see pages 30–33). Use a no. 2 nozzle to pipe three rows of 'pearls' in white royal icing around the base of the mini cakes, gradually making the 'pearls' smaller. Stand each cake on an upturned glass or small bowl to make access to the bottom of the cake easier.

two Change to a no. 1.5 nozzle and ice a fourth layer of 'pearls', leaving a gap between each one. Leave to dry. Stand the large cake on one of the 20 cm (8 inch) drums and decorate it in the same way.

one

two three Dilute the pearl dust in alcohol and paint the 'pearls'.

Variation These mini cakes would make an ideal favour or leaving gift. They look great boxed with tissue paper and tied up with ribbon and will be so much more appreciated by your guests than the usual slice of cake.

four

four Use royal icing to fasten the polystyrene block to the largest drum, then stack the other drums, in descending order of size. Arrange the mini cakes in three layers, of ten, eight and five cakes, with the large cake on top. Fasten ribbon around the edges of all the cake drums, holding the ends in position with glue. Decorate the finished cake with in-season flowers, arranging them in the gaps between the mini cakes and on top of the large cake.

Venetian Carnival

I'm afraid we have decided the theme of your next party: the Venice Carnival. This cake is amazingly easy to make, and you can decorate your mask in any way you like with edible glitter, lustre or colours. You can buy a mould for the mask from a party or art shop. You will need to allow a couple of days to make this cake, so that the different layers of petal paste, royal icing and dye have time to dry thoroughly.

Ingredients

20 cm (8 inch) square cake, 7 cm (3 inches) deep

900 g (1 lb 13 oz) white sugarpaste

200 g (7 oz) white petal paste

red edible dye

edible gold dust

clear alcohol

250 g (8 oz) royal icing

pearl dust

blue and yellow edible dye

To assemble the cake

40 cm (16 inch) square cake drum

rolling pin

mask and headdress templates (see pages 154–5)

mould (see above)

sharp knife

kitchen paper or tissue paper

bone shaping tool

'fabric-effect' rolling pin

piping bag and no. 2 nozzle

no. 1 paintbrush

no. 2 paintbrush

gold-painted wooden dowel

15 mm (¾ inch) wide dark red ribbon

edible glue

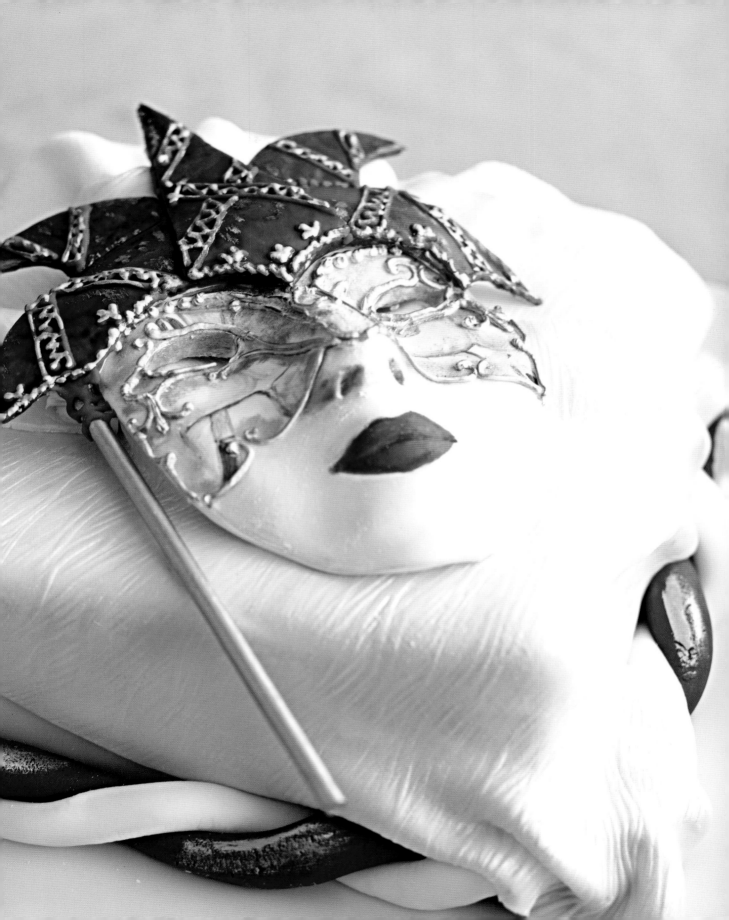

one

two

three

one Cover the cake drum and cake with white sugarpaste (see pages 30–33). Make the mask by rolling out the petal paste to about 4 mm (¼ inch) deep, place the template on the paste and cut around it.

two Mark the positions of the eyes and mouth with a knife, remove the template and cut out the eyes.

three Place the mould on a firm surface and make sure it is padded with kitchen paper or tissue paper so that it does not give way and distort the mask. Carefully lift the sugarpaste mask and place it over the mould and gently press the sugarpaste into shape. Use a bone shaping tool to press in the nostrils and mouth.

four

four Roll out more white petal paste and use the template (see page 154) to cut out the headdress. Brush the top of the petal paste mask with a little cooled boiled water and stick the headdress in position, supporting the overhang with a piece of foam or crumpled tissue paper. Leave the headdress and mask to dry for 24 hours.

five Roll out about 250 g (8 oz) each of white and red sugarpaste to 15 mm (¾ inch) sausages, about 80 cm (32 inches) long, and twist them together to form a rope. Attach this around the base of the iced cake with a little hot water.

six

six Cut the ends of the rope at angles so that they butt neatly together at the back of the cake and press them together.

seven Roll out some white petal paste to about 2 mm (less than $\frac{1}{8}$ inch) thick and about 25 cm (10 inches) square. Use a 'fabric-effect' rolling pin to emboss the surface, then gently drape it over the cake at an angle, arranging the folds at the corners to resemble fabric. Highlight parts of the rope with a little gold dust mixed with clear alcohol.

seven

eight
Pipe the details of the decoration with royal icing and a no. 2 nozzle. Paint the headdress dark red.

nine

ten

eleven Carefully lift the sugarpaste mask into position on the iced cake, securing it in place with a little royal icing. Attach the gold-painted wooden dowel with edible glue and pipe more details around the base. Leave to dry. Secure the ribbon around the edge of the drum and glue the ends in place.

nine Paint over the piped details with gold dust. Leave to dry, then use a soft paintbrush to apply pearl dust to the lower part of the face.

ten Paint the lips red, then use blue and yellow edible dyes to colour in sections of the mask.

Marie Antoinette Macaroon Tower

The extravagant queen of France loved pastries, and it's often, if wrongly, said that she suggested to the hungry crowds of Paris that if they were hungry, they should eat cakes. This creation is dedicated to her: the queen who wasn't in touch with her people but who did have great taste in cakes. The macaroons are quite rich, so I generally use a dummy cake as the base of this cake, but if you prefer you could use a sponge or fruit cake, covered in sugarpaste.

Ingredients

60 macaroons (see page 21)

800 g (1 lb 10 oz) white sugarpaste

250 g (8 oz) white chocolate

royal icing

sugar silver balls, to decorate

200 g (7 oz) chocolate ganache (see page 28)
  or vanilla buttercream (see page 24)
  or raspberry jam

To assemble the cake

23 cm (9 inches) round polystyrene cake
  dummy, 8 cm (7½ inches) deep

23 cm (9 inches) round cake card

pastry brush

polystyrene cone, 20 cm (8 in) in diameter

piping bag and no. 1 nozzle

flat serving plate

tweezers

two

one

three

one Place the cake or polystyrene dummy on a cake card and cover with white sugarpaste. You can also make the macaroons the day before and store them in an airtight container. Sandwich them together with your preferred filling at the last minute or they will go soggy. Melt the chocolate in a heatproof bowl set over a pan of simmering water or in a microwave in two 20-second bursts on 'high' (be careful because white chocolate burns quickly). Use a pastry brush to coat the cone in a fine layer of chocolate and leave it to set in the refrigerator for about 15 minutes. Keep the remaining melted chocolate warm so that it does not set.

two Fill a small piping bag and a no. 1 nozzle with white royal icing and pipe two rows of delicate swags around the edge of the dummy. Turn a soup plate upside down on a work surface and place another flat serving plate on top to create a 'turntable'. Sit the dummy on top of this to make it easier. Now add the sugar balls. For precision, use tweezers to add the balls: if you are nervous the heat from your hands will cause the gilding to disappear.

three Pipe a row of 'pearls' in white icing to help attach the cake to the plate.

four Secure the cone to the centre of the dummy with a little royal icing. Leave it to set for a few minutes. Meanwhile, fill the macaroons and brush a little of the remaining melted chocolate on to each one to secure them to the cone. You will find it easiest to work your way up from the bottom to the top.

five Finally, secure three macaroons at angles in a triangle and place one last macaroon on top of them.

Variation This will be a great centrepiece for any celebration. Guests can help themselves directly from the stand, or the macaroons can be placed on trays and served later on with coffee. But, of course, you don't have to build this type of creation to create an impression. You could simply present loose macaroons in decorated boxes or bags as hostess gifts or wedding favours.

four

five

Delicate Daisies

This pretty design is perfect for a birthday celebration or a girls' get-together for a baby shower. The colours could be reversed so you have pink flowers on a white cake or you could experiment with different colours altogether. You can buy sets of blossom cutters in different sizes.

Ingredients

15 cm (6 inch) round cake, 8 cm (3 inches) deep

20 cm (8 inch) round cake, 8 cm (3 inches deep)

1.1 kg (2 lb 4 oz) pale pink sugarpaste (or white sugarpaste coloured with edible dye)

200 g (7 oz) white petal paste

pink royal icing

To assemble the cake

25 cm (10 inch) round cake drum

30 cm (12 inch) round cake drum

15 cm (6 inch) cake card

4 dowel rods

15 mm (³/₄ inch) wide pink ribbon

edible glue or a gluestick

rolling pin

blossom cutters

foam pad

balling tool

piping bag and no. 2 nozzle

one

one Place the 15 cm (6 inch) cake on a cake card. Cover the cake drums and cakes in pale pink sugarpaste and stack them (see pages 30–35). Fasten ribbon around the bottom of each cake and around the drums, securing the ends in place with glue. Roll out some petal paste and use different sized blossom cutters to cut out the flowers.

two

two Transfer the flowers to a foam pad and use a balling tool to curve each petal. Leave them to dry.

three Attach the petals to the cake with pink royal icing, arranging the largest flowers in a garland shape round the top of each tier, with the smaller flowers 'draped' down the sides at regular intervals.

three

four Pipe little pink balls of royal icing into the centre of each flower to finish.

Exquisite Jewels

The simplicity of the cake combined with the beauty and lightness of the wired crystals make this into a stunning centrepiece, worthy of the grandest of occasions. The wired crystals are available in strips, but these will not always be long enough to go all the way round the cakes, so use shorter pieces to fill the gaps.

Ingredients

10 cm (4 inch) round cake, 20 cm (4 inches) deep

15 cm (6 inch) round cake, 20 cm (4 inches) deep

20 cm (8 inch) round cake, 20 cm (4 inches) deep

1.5 kg (3 lb) white sugarpaste

250 g (8 oz) white royal icing

To assemble the cake

25 cm (10 inch) diameter cake drum

30 cm (12 inch) diameter cake drum

10 cm (4 inch) round cake card

15 cm (6 inch) round cake card

8 dowel rods

strips of wired crystals

piping bag and no. 2 nozzle

florists' pins

tweezers

15 mm (¾ inch) wide ribbon

edible glue or a gluestick

one

two

one Place the two smaller cakes on cake cards. Cover the cake drums and cakes with white sugarpaste and stack them (see pages 30–35). Cut and bend the strips of wired crystal to fit each tier, using shorter bits to fill any gaps.

two Use a piping bag and no. 2 nozzle to dot some white royal icing around the base of each tier.

three Secure the crystal strips with florists' pins, pressing them gently into the cake. Leave to dry.

three

four

four

Use tweezers and your fingers to arrange the crystals until you are happy with them. Carefully remove the florists' pins, then fasten ribbon around the drums, securing the ends in place with edible glue.

Variation This chic idea can be adapted to suit individual mini cakes. If you are using only a few, the wired crystals can be pushed directly into the top of the cake. To give more support if you are using anumber of wired crystals, you can first push a small posy pick into the top of each cake. Remember to finish off the base of each cake with a ribbon.

Designer Handbag

If you can't afford the real thing, try making one of your favourite designer's handbag from cake. It will be the perfect present for a special friend or the ideal centrepiece for an afternoon tea. For larger parties, you could make a number of different bags and group them on a drum or, for a real challenge, you could make small versions as party favours – a different one for each guest.

Ingredients

20 cm (8 inch) square cake, 8 cm (3 inches) deep

100 g (3½ oz) pale blue sugarpaste

250 g (8 oz) buttercream (see page 24)

1.25 g (2 lb 8 oz) white sugarpaste

50 g (2 oz) white petal paste

125 g (4 oz) ivory royal icing

pink and blue and clear pearl dust clear alcohol

To assemble the cake

30 cm (12 inch) round cake drum

15 mm (¾ inch) wide pale blue ribbon

edible glue or a gluestick

large sharp serrated knife

sharp knife

rolling pin

soft paintbrush

quilting tool or stitch marker

2 x no. 22 white wires

petal cutter

foam pad

ball tool

piping bag and no. 2 nozzle

tweezers

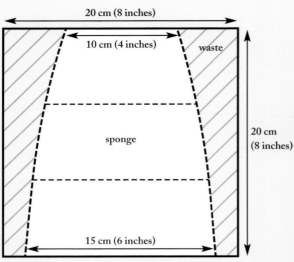

20 cm (8 inches)

10 cm (4 inches)

waste

20 cm (8 inches)

sponge

15 cm (6 inches)

Diagram 1

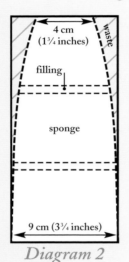

4 cm (1¾ inches)

waste

filling

sponge

9 cm (3¾ inches)

Diagram 2

one Ice the drum with pale blue sugarpaste and cut out a hole for the cake in the centre and attach ribbon around the edge of the drum, securing the ends in place with glue. Cut up the cake as shown in diagram 1.

two Use buttercream to sandwich the cake pieces back together, one on top of the other. Using a sharp serrated knife, cut the cake into a handbag shape as shown in diagram 2 and cover the outside with buttercream. Roll out the white sugarpaste and cut out two triangles to fit the side of the bag. Apply to the cake and trim to fit. Cut two more large pieces to fit the front and the back of the bag. Cut another smaller piece to form a flap, 16 cm (6½ inches) long by 8 cm (3⅓ inches) wide.

three Brush the front of the bag with cooled boiled water and attach the flap, smoothing all over with the flat of your hand and paying particular attention to the join between the flap and the back of the bag.

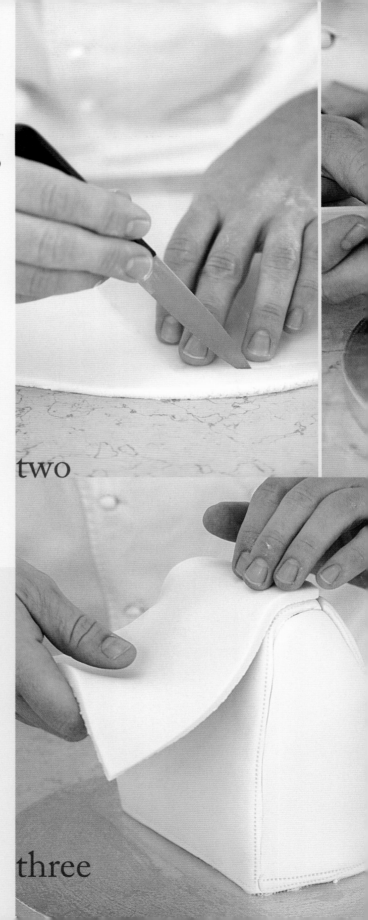

two

three

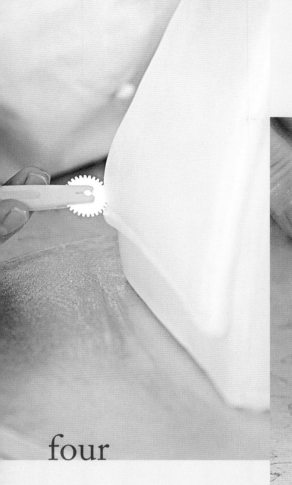

four

four Use a quilting tool to emboss stitching around the edge of the bag and flap.

five Make the handle by rolling out a fairly thick strip of petal paste 30 x 6 cm (12 x 2½ inches). Place two no. 22 white wires in the centre of the strip so that they overhang the ends of the strip by about 5 cm (2 inches) at each end. Dampen the strip slightly with cooled boiled water.

five

six

seven

six Fold one side of the handle over the wires, press down and smooth it with your fingers. Trim away the excess petal paste.

seven Squeeze the sides to smooth the joints and run the quilting tool along both edges.

eight Bend over the handle to fit the top of the bag and leave it to dry.

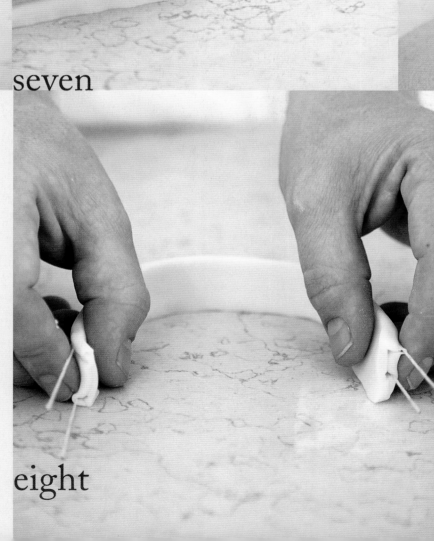

eight

nine

nine When the handle is dry, secure it in position by sticking the wires into the side seams at the top of the bag.

ten Cut side pieces out of petal paste, shaped like a square above an inverted triangle, and add stitches along the edges of the square, with a diagonal cross inside, and along the edges of the triangle. Secure the pieces over the ends of the handle with a little cooled boiled water.

eleven Carefully transfer the cake to the drum, then make the flower. Roll out some petal paste very thinly and use a petal cutter to cut out six petals. Place them on a foam pad and use a ball tool to shape the edges.

twelve Pipe a small ball of ivory royal icing on to the centre of the flap and attach a petal, holding it in place for a few seconds until the icing sets. Pipe another little dot of icing and attach another petal, overlapping the first slightly. Continue attaching the remaining petals in the same way.

thirteen Roll a small ball of petal paste. Pipe a small ball of royal icing in the centre of the flower and use your fingers or tweezers to attach the petal paste ball to the centre of flower.

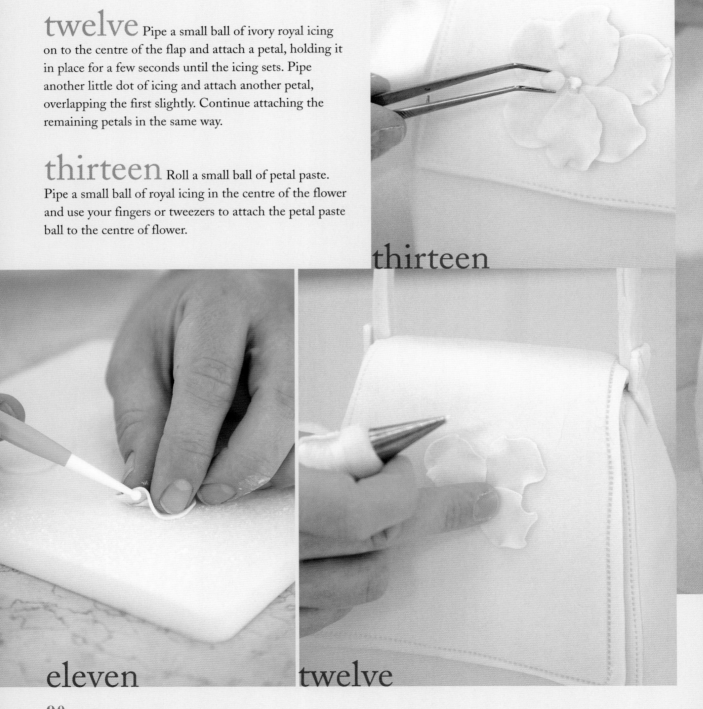

thirteen

eleven   twelve

fifteen Paint the flower with pink pearl dust, then add some highlights with blue pearl dust (you can cover the drum with kitchen paper or a piece of greaseproof paper to protect it, if you like).

fourteen

fourteen Use a soft brush to paint the bag with pearl dust mixed with a little clear alcohol.

Toile de Jouy

A classic French wall-covering inspired this romantic design. Toile de Jouy has enjoyed something of a revival in the last few years, and it's used for fabrics, greetings cards, lampshades ... and now as a wedding cake. Even if you're not artistically inclined, you will find this stunning centrepiece is not too difficult to re-create, although it will take several days to make and decorate. The traditional Toile de Jouy colours are black, red, pink and blue, but you could use wallpaper, fabric or an idea from a pattern book for your cake. This cake will look best if you use square, deep cakes to give plenty of space for the drawing. Fruit cake is especially well suited to this recipe.

Ingredients

- 15 cm (6 inch) square cake, 10 cm (4 inches) deep
- 20 cm (8 inch) square cake, 10 cm (4 inches) deep
- 25 cm (10 inch) square cake, 10 cm (4 inches) deep
- 30 cm (12 inch) square cake, 10 cm (4 inches) deep
- 4.4 kg (8 lb 10 oz) marzipan
- 5.3 kg (10 lb 15 oz) sugarpaste

To assemble the cake

- 40 cm (16 inch) square cake drum
- 45 cm (18 inch) square cake drum
- 15 cm (6 inch) square cake card
- 20 cm (8 inch) square cake card
- 25 cm (10 inch) square cake card
- 16 dowel rods
- tracing paper
- design of your choice
- florists' or dressmakers' pins
- food colouring pens
- 1.5 cm (¾ inch) wide black ribbon
- edible glue or a gluestick

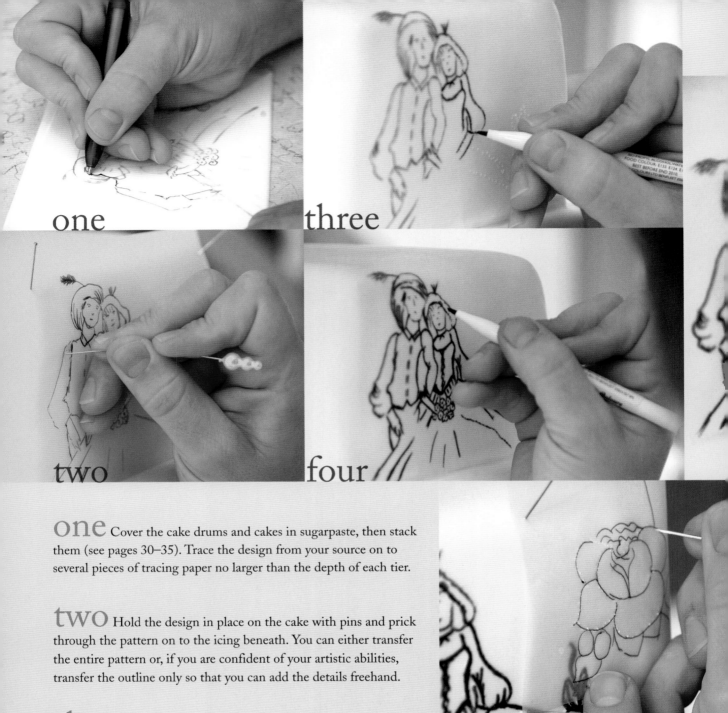

one

three

two

four

five

one Cover the cake drums and cakes in sugarpaste, then stack them (see pages 30–35). Trace the design from your source on to several pieces of tracing paper no larger than the depth of each tier.

two Hold the design in place on the cake with pins and prick through the pattern on to the icing beneath. You can either transfer the entire pattern or, if you are confident of your artistic abilities, transfer the outline only so that you can add the details freehand.

three Fill in the design with a fine food colouring pen.

four Build up the design, going over the details with a thicker pen if you wish.

five Prick on further parts of the design as you go.

Variation Take your time. This cake requires a lot of patience, and because the design is worked in black and white you really can't afford to make any mistakes. Food colouring pens don't drip, but you could use a fine paintbrush and edible food dye if you felt confident. To avoid smudging your work, you could draw the outlines then fill in the detail when they have dried. We have used this idea on individual cakes, and they looked lovely, too. The rose motif worked particularly well in red.

six

SiX This outline will give you a framework to use when filling in the details. Attach ribbon around the base of each cake stacked tier, finishing with a flat bow at the front and neatly trimming at the ends. Secure with pins. Fasten ribbon around the edges of the cake drums, securing the ends in place with edible glue or a gluestick.

Butterfly Tower

This beautifully romantic display would be perfect for a country wedding. Your guests will appreciate being able to take these special keepsakes home with them. You can colour the butterflies any shades you wish – we used blue, green, pink and yellow and added a little lustre to the edges of their wings.

Ingredients

18 x 5 cm (2 inch) round cakes, 7 cm (3 inches) deep

3.75 g (7 lb 8 oz) white sugarpaste

500 g (1 lb) royal icing

200 g (7 oz) petal paste

edible dyes, both liquid and powder, in colours of your choice

petal dust, in colours of your choice

To assemble the cake

15 cm (6 inch) round cake drum

20 cm (8 inch) round cake drum

25 cm (10 inch) round cake drum

18 x 5 cm (2 inch) round cake cards

15 mm (³/₄ inch) wide ribbon

edible glue or a gluestick

7 cm (3 inch) polystyrene block, (4 inches) deep

10 cm (4 inch) polystyrene block, (4 inches) deep

rolling pin

butterfly cutter

small pieces of foam

ball tool

no. 2 paintbrush

soft brush

greaseproof paper

plastic flower stamens (to use for antennae)

tweezers

one

one Cover the cakes and drums with white sugarpaste. Place each mini cake on a cake card. Attach ribbon around the base of each cake and drum, securing the ends together with glue. Use a little royal icing to hold polystyrene blocks in the centre of the two largest cake drums. Stack the drums. Colour the petal paste with powder and roll it out. Use cutters to cut out about 24 butterflies. Remember to cover all spare petal paste with clingfilm so that it does not dry out.

two Rest the butterflies on a piece of foam and use a ball tool to create indentations along the edges of the wings to give them shape.

two

three

three Hold the wings at different angles with pieces of foam and leave them to dry.

four Paint details on the wings with a fine paintbrush in a colour to complement the petal paste.

four

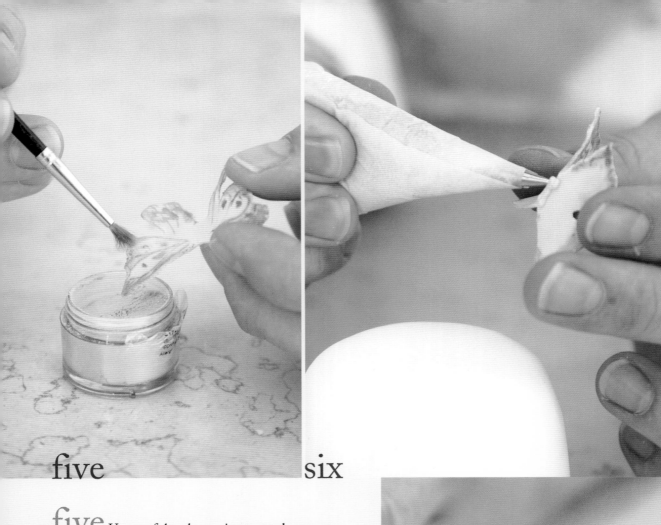

five   six

five Use a soft brush to paint a complementary colour petal dust on to the wings.

six Divide the royal icing into as many parts as colours you are using and colour it to match the butterflies. Make a piping bag from a piece of greaseproof paper, fill it with royal icing in a colour to complement the butterfly and snip the end off the bag. Use the icing to attach the butterflies to the top and sides of the cakes.

seven Using the rest of the coloured icing, pipe a zigzag line up the butterflies' bodies and add a blob for the heads.

seven

eight

eight Attach plastic flower stamens for antennae and hold them in position in the royal icing with tweezers until set. Arrange the cakes, with eight at the bottom, six in the centre and four at the top.

Red Berry Romance

This unusual design is a perfect alternative to anything with icing. It is appropriate for all kinds of celebration and can be used on tiered or stacked cakes. The crunchiness of the chocolate cigars is the perfect counterpart to the lovely soft filling. It can, of course, be made with dark or milk chocolate as an alternative.

Ingredients

150 g (5 oz) white chocolate, melted

20 cm (8 inch) round marquise cake, 9 cm (3$\frac{1}{2}$ inches) deep (see page 16)

white chocolate ganache (see page 28)

2 x 700 g (about 1$\frac{1}{2}$ lb) boxes white chocolate cigarillos

white modelling chocolate (see page 29)

icing sugar, to dust

in-season fruit, such as redcurrants, raspberries and strawberries, to decorate

To assemble the cake

30 cm (12 inch) round drum

15 mm ($\frac{3}{4}$ inch) wide white ribbon

edible glue or a gluestick

palette knife

fan mould

small sharp knife

1 m 30 cm x 5 cm (52 x 2 inch) wide dark purple velvet ribbon

one

two

one Cover the cake drum with a thin layer of melted white chocolate (see page 30). Attach ribbon around the edge of the drum, securing the ends with edible glue or a gluestick. Position the cake in the centre of the drum and use a palette knife to cover it with a thick layer of melted white chocolate ganache.

two Working quickly, before the ganache sets, stick white chocolate cigarillos around the outside of the cake. If necessary, cut one in half to fill a gap at the back.

three Roll out the modelling chocolate thinly and make the fans by placing the mould over the chocolate. Press it down firmly with your fingers, then lift the modelling chocolate off the mould.

four Dust your work surface with icing sugar. Put the modelling chocolate on your work surface and cut out the fans with a small knife. Leave the fans to dry.

three

four

five

six

five Use a small palette knife to cover sections of the top of the cake with melted white chocolate ganache. Press fans on to the surface of the cake, overlapping them as you work around the edge then inwards in a spiral towards the centre.

six Fasten a velvet ribbon around the cake. Dip the fruits into melted white chocolate and arrange them around the top of the cake.

seven Arrange some whole and halved fruits around the base of the cake, then dust them lightly with icing sugar.

seven

Peony Perfection

If you've ever wanted to be an artist, this is your chance. The stacked cakes are decorated with hand-painted peonies, and the bold colours of the flowers make this an eye-catching design. Take your time, allowing each colour to dry properly before you add the next.

Ingredients

15 cm (6 inch) square cake, 10 cm (4 inches) deep

20 cm (8 inch) square cake, 10 cm (4 inches) deep

25 cm (10 inch) square cake, 10 cm (4 inches) deep

3 kg (6 lb) blue sugarpaste *or* white sugarpaste coloured with ice blue edible dye

500 g (1 lb) blue royal icing *or* white royal icing coloured with ice blue edible dye

colouring powders in super white, rose pink and deep pink

To assemble the cake

35 cm (14 inch) square cake drum

40 cm (16 inch) square cake drum

15 cm (6 inch) square cake card

20 cm (8 inch) square cake card

piping bag and no. 3 nozzle

food colouring pen

no. 1 and no. 2 paintbrushes

scribe or fine needle (if design is traced)

tracing paper

15 mm (³⁄₄ inch) wide blue ribbon

edible glue or a gluestick

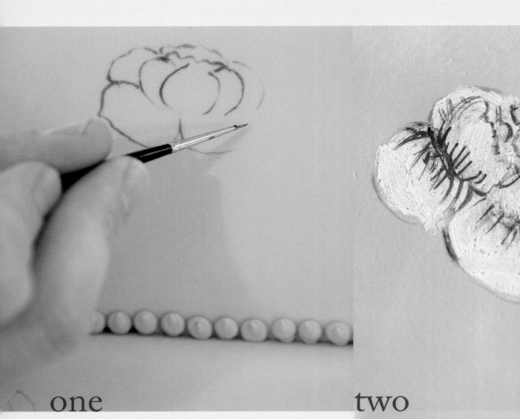

one

two

one Cover the cake drums and cakes with blue sugarpaste and stack them (see pages 30–35) Using royal icing, pipe a series of little 'pearls' around the base of each cake. Leave the icing to dry for about one hour. If you are confident to do so, draw the peony design on to the cake with a deep pink fine food colouring pen or paintbrush and deep pink coluring powder mixed with a little cooled boiled water. Alternatively, follow step two.

two Trace the pattern given here, following the instructions given for Toile de Jouy (see pages 92–5).

three Mix the colour for the flowers, using super white powder, a touch of rose pink and a little cooled boiled water. Fill in the shapes with a soft no. 2 paintbrush and leave to dry.

three

five Use rose pink to add short lines to the top of the area you have just painted in pink. Attach ribbon to the drums, securing the ends with edible glue or a gluestick.

four

four Use a no. 1 paintbrush to highlight the petals and the heart of each flower with a darker shade of pink. Leave to dry.

Dotty Heart

There are always occasions when a heart-shaped cake is needed, such as Valentine's Day, wedding anniversaries or engagement parties. You will also sometimes want to make a cake for those special moments when you want to show someone that you love them.

Ingredients

10 cm (4 inch) heart-shaped cake, 8 cm (3 inches) deep

20 cm (8 inch) heart-shaped cake, 8 cm (3 inches) deep

1.1 kg (2 lb 1½ oz)white sugarpaste

pale yellow food dye

500 g (1 lb) white royal icing

fresh or crystallized flower petals, to decorate

To assemble the cake

30 cm (12 inch) round cake drum

35 cm (14 inch) round cake drum

10 cm (4 inch) round cake card cut into a heart shape

15 mm (¾ inch) wide pale yellow ribbon

edible glue or a gluestick

piping bag and no. 2 nozzle

pearl dust

clear alcohol

one Colour the sugarpaste pale yellow, use it to cover the cake drums and cakes, then stack them (see pages 30–35). Attach ribbon to the cake drums, securing the ends in position with edible glue or a gluestick. Using royal icing, pipe a series of little 'pearls' around the base of each cake.

one

two

two Use a no. 2 nozzle to pipe dots of white royal icing evenly over the cakes.

three
Be careful to keep the dots evenly spaced across all surfaces of the cake. Leave the icing to dry.

four

four
Dilute some pearl dust with alcohol and pearlize the icing dots. If liked, decorate the top of the cake with fresh or crystallized petals. Burnt orange flowers work well with the yellow sugarpaste. If using roses, gently tease out the petals with your fingers.

Baroque Splendour

This lovely cake will be a wonderful centrepiece at any table. The guests will be able to enjoy eating the marzipan fruits as well as the delicious cake itself. For a wedding, you could make a tiered cake with four cakes, 36 cm (14 inches), 25 cm (10 inches), 15 cm (6 inches) and 8 cm (3 inches) across, and each 12 cm (5 inches) deep. Decorate them with piped swags and fleur-de-lis and arrange the fruits around the base of each tier and on top of the smallest cake.

Ingredients

15 cm (6 inch) round cake, 10 cm (4 inches) deep

500 g (1 lb) white sugarpaste

500 g (1 lb) white royal icing

700 g (about 1½ lb) marzipan

yellow, green and red edible liquid dyes

dust food colour

To assemble the cake

25 cm (10 inch) cake drum

15 mm (¾ inch) wide white ribbon

edible glue or a gluestick

piping bag and no. 2 and no. 3 nozzles

broad leaf nozzle

marzipan roller

marzipan fruit moulds

no. 2 paintbrush

pearl dust

clear alcohol

edible gold paint

one

two

one Cover the cake drum and cake with white
sugarpaste (see pages 30 and 33). Attach ribbon to the
cake drums, securing the ends in position with glue. Place
the cake on the drum and use sugarpaste to make little pear
shapes and attach them to the icing with cooled boiled water.
These form the basis of the bunches of grapes.

two Use a no. 2 nozzle and white royal icing to
pipe little spheres from the pointed end of the pearl
shapes, building them up to form a bunch of grapes.
(Add vine leaves with a broad leaf nozzle-check pics).
Leave the icing to dry.

three Use a no. 2 nozzle and white royal icing
to pipe little 'pearls' around the base of the cake.

three

four

five

four Use a no. 3 nozzle to pipe the fleur-de-lis decoration around the side of the cake.

five Change to a no. 2 nozzle to pipe the 'pearls' in the centre of the design. Leave the icing to dry.

six Knead edible dye into the marzipan to colour it as appropriate for the different fruits – yellow for lemons, green for limes and so on.

seven

seven Roll out the marzipan to the correct thickness using the spacers provided with a special marzipan roller.

eight Use the cutters provided to cut different fruit shapes out of the marzipan and place them in the roller.

nine Use the roller to mould the shapes into fruits. The roller should come with instructions.

ten Apply dust food colour to highlight the fruits and give the impression of texture and bloom.

eleven Dilute a little pearl dust in alcohol and paint the grapes and fleur-de-lis patterns across the whole cake.

twelve Arrange the marzipan fruits around the base of the cake and pile them on top, holding them in position with some royal icing.

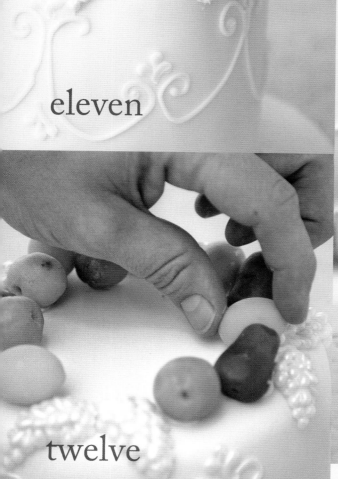

eleven

twelve

thirteen Apply some liquid gold with a no. 2 brush to some of the piped decoration and to the tops of the fruits.

Lavender Fields

This creative design will bring back memories of the herb-covered landscapes of the south of France. All that is missing is the relaxing fragrance of the fresh lavender. As an alternative you could try piping lily of the valley on to pale blue or ivory sugarpaste or try snow drops or cherry blossom – any delicate flower would look lovely.

Ingredients

24 x 5 cm (2 inch) square cakes, 6 cm (2½ inches) deep

5.5 kg (1 lb 1½ oz) white sugarpaste

700g (1 lb 6½ oz) royal icing

green and lavender liquid edible dye

To assemble the cake

24 x 5 cm (2 inch) square cake cards

15 cm (6 inch) square cake drum

23 cm (9 inch) square cake drum

30 cm (12 inch) square cake drum

piping bag and no. 1 and no. 1.5 or no. 2 nozzle

no. 0 paintbrush

15 cm (6 inch) round or square polystyrene block, 6 cm (2½ inches) deep

10 cm (4 inch) round or square polystyrene block, 6 cm (2½ inches) deep

15 mm (¾ inch) wide lavender ribbon

edible glue or a gluestick

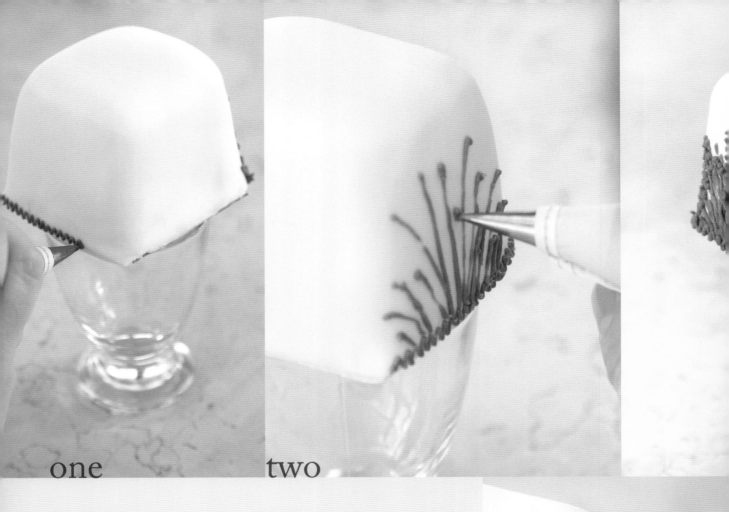

one

two

one Place the cakes on to cake cards. Cover the cake drums and the individual cakes with white sugarpaste (see pages 30–33). Make some green royal icing and use a no. 1 nozzle to pipe a line of short grass along the sides of the cakes.

two Next pipe green lavender stalks up the sides of the cakes. Leave the icing to dry.

three Pipe another layer of squiggles of grass up the sides of the cakes to cover the base of the stalks.

three

five Set one polystyrene block in the centre of the large cake drum, holding it in position with a little royal icing, and surround it with cakes. Rest the second drum on the block, holding it in place with royal icing; set the remaining block in the centre and surround it with cakes. Place the final drum on top of the block, again securing it with royal icing, and arrange four cakes in the centre. Fasten ribbon around the drums, securing the ends in position with edible glue or a gluestick.

five

four

four Make some lavender royal icing and use a no. 1.5 or no. 2 nozzle to pipe the lavender flowers. Delicately touch the wet icing with the tip of a paintbrush to flatten any spiky bits.

Croquembouche

This French cake is traditionally made to celebrate a christening, a first communion or a wedding. We've given it a modern twist by creating several smaller versions for individual tables to share and enjoy. The second batch of caramel is used as spun sugar to decorate the finished arrangement.

Ingredients

45 choux buns (see page 20)

750 g (1 lb 8 oz) crème patissière (see page 25)

2 quantities caramel (see page 27), made separately

To assemble the cake

small sharp knife

piping bag and no. 4 nozzle

baking sheet or greaseproof paper

7 cm (3 inch) round polystyrene block, 10 cm (4 inches) deep

plate or cake stand

2 forks

edible gold leaf

one

one Use a small knife to make a hole in the top of each bun.

two Fill a piping bag with crème patissière and use a no. 4 nozzle to fill the buns.

three Carefully dip the bottom of each bun into the first batch of the caramel then transfer them to a lightly oiled baking sheet or greaseproof paper. Press down slightly on to the surface and leave to dry for about 5 minutes.

two   three

five Stick a further row of buns in position, placing them on the inside edge of the row below and positioning them so that they tilt slightly inwards. If you cannot fit a whole bun in to finish a row, use a sharp knife to trim a little off the adjacent buns to make room for the final one.

four

four Place a circular block in the centre of a plate and surround it with buns, dipping them into more caramel so that they stick in place. Add a second row in the same way, holding each bun in place until it sticks, then carefully remove the polystyrene block.

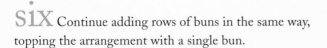

six

six Continue adding rows of buns in the same way, topping the arrangement with a single bun.

seven Hold two forks back to back and dip them into the second batch of caramel. Spin the caramel in circles around and over the buns, separating the forks to make longer trails. Caramel strands that trail over the edge of the plate can be broken off by your fingers or with a knife. You can also use your fingers to tease out strands of caramel and position them on the buns.

seven

To make a traditional, large croquembouche, line the inside of a special croquembouche mould with greased foil. Fill it to the top with the filled, dipped buns, dripping on hot caramel as you go to act as glue, then invert and remove the mould carefully so that the conical pile of buns stands on a plate. Decorate with caramel as above. To serve as below, dip in caramel and then immediately in caster sugar.

eight

eight Hold a sheet of gold leaf close to the croquembouche and use a sharp knife to scrape tiny pieces of gold leaf off the sheet and on to the caramel.

Glossy Ganache

This smooth chocolate ganache-coated cake is given a modern look by the addition of a transparent cube holding fresh flowers. Instead of flowers, you could decorate this cake with fresh berries for a summer celebration or with mixed nuts for an autumn event. A round cake will look just as good on a filled glass cylinder.

Ingredients

15 cm (6 inch) square chocolate cake, 10 cm (4 inches) deep

20 cm (8 inch) square chocolate cake, 10 cm (4 inches) deep

250 g (8 oz) plain dark chocolate, melted

2 quantities dark chocolate ganache (see page 28)

fresh flowers to decorate (we used gloriosa lilies)

To assemble the cake

25 cm (10 inch) square cake drum

30 cm (12 inch) square cake drum

15 cm (6 inch) square cake card

soft brush

15 mm (¾ inch) wide brown ribbon

wire rack

palette knife

5 dowel rods

piping bag and no. 1.5 nozzle

Up to 10 posy picks

30 cm (12 inch) square glass or Perspex container

one

two

three

one Brush the cake drums with dark chocolate. Stand the cakes on a wire rack and flat plate to catch any drips. Carefully melt the ganache and use it to coat the tops and sides of both cakes.

two Smooth the ganache with a palette knife and leave it to set. When the chocolate on the drum is dry, attach the brown ribbon using edible glue or a gluestick.

three When it is set, lift the larger cake into the centre of the drum. Put the smaller cake on the cake card. Push four dowel rods into the cake and trim them to length (see page 34). Brush the area of the larger cake within the dowel rods with a little melted ganache and place the smaller cake on top, making sure the card rests on the dowel rods.

four

five

four Use a no. 1.5 nozzle to pipe some chocolate 'pearls' around the base of each tier using the remaining ganache.

five Stick posy picks into the top of the cake, cut the stems of the flowers and insert them into the picks.

six Stick further posy picks into the cake where you want to add flowers, cutting stems and inserting as above. Fill a glass or Perspex container with fresh petals or flowers and place the cake on top, so that the cake drum rests on the container.

six

American Retro

The inspiration for this stylish, almost kitsch, design came from a greetings card showing an American kitchen goddess making some of these cakes. The velvet and satin ribbons give the cake a feminine look. We used three different types of cake – lemon for the top, chocolate in the middle and fruit at the bottom – for the tiers, but you could use whatever types of cake you prefer. To avoid a Leaning Tower of Pisa effect, use a small spirit level (available from DIY stores) at every stage as you build up the cake.

Ingredients

15 cm (6 inch) round cake, 8 cm (3 inches) deep

20 cm (8 inch) round cake, 8 cm (3 inches) deep

25 cm (10 inch) round cake, 8 cm (3 inches) deep

3 kg (6 lb) light pink sugarpaste *or* white sugarpaste coloured with shell pink edible dye

500 g (1 lb) chocolate brown royal icing *or* white royal icing coloured with chocolate brown liquid dye

To assemble the cake

20 cm (8 inch) round cake card

30 cm (12 inch) round cake drum

35 cm (14 inch) round cake drum

15 cm (6 inch) round cake card

8 dowel rods

15 mm (³/₄ inch) wide light pink ribbon

edible glue or a gluestick

3 cm (1¼ inch) wide dark brown velvet ribbon

florists' or dressmakers' pins

piping bag and no. 1.5 nozzle

one Cover the cake drums and cakes with pink
sugarpaste. Place the largest cake on the cake drum
then stack the other two cakes on top, finishing with
the smallest cake. Attach some of the pink ribbon to
each drum using edible glue or a gluestick. Attach the
brown velvet ribbon around the base of each tier,
trimming the ends of the ribbon neatly and fastening
them in position with a pin.

two

two Add the pink satin ribbon over the velvet one, tying a bow on the centre of each tier, and making sure that they align at the front of the cake.

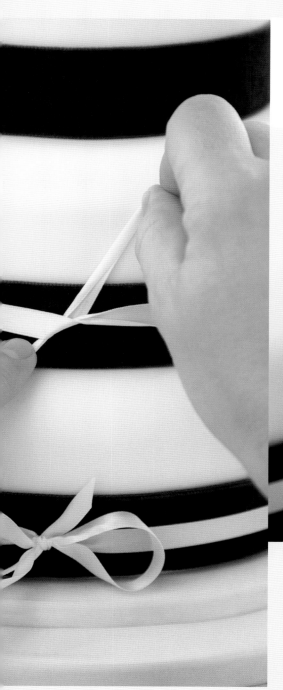

three

three Fill a piping bag with chocolate-brown royal icing. Starting just above the ribbon and using a no. 1.5 nozzle pipe tiny dots at regular intervals around the first tier. Add dots to the other two tiers and leave to dry overnight. If you prefer, use a tape measure and a scribe or sharp needle to prick holes where the dots will go to give an even pattern.

Heavenly Cherub
& Roses

This rococo creation is made entirely of white chocolate.
It would be the perfect end of a special meal or celebration.
The filling is summery, but you could use any filling that you
prefer. We used a white chocolate marquise (see page 16),
but you could use any type of cake you like and cover it with
cream-coloured sugarpaste so that it looks as if it is covered
with white chocolate. Cherub moulds are available from
sugarcraft shops.

Ingredients

20 cm (8 inch) round cake, 12 cm
   (5 inches) deep
(575 g (1 lb 2½ oz) cream sugarpaste –
   optional)
500 g (1 lb) white chocolate, melted
200 g (7 oz) modelling chocolate
berry fruits to decorate

To assemble the cake

30 cm (12 inch) round cake card or drum
cherub mould
clingfilm
rose leaf cutter
fan mould
palette knife
cake stand

one

two

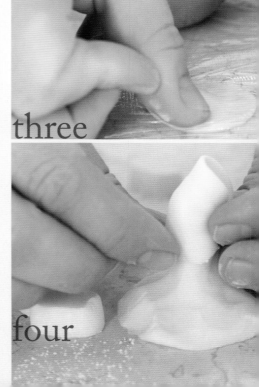

three

four

one If you are covering a cake in sugarpaste, ice it onto a cake drum. If using a marquise, finish off the cake with a layer of white chocolate and place it on a cake card. Make the cherub by pouring melted chocolate into a mould. Tap the full mould sharply on your work surface to remove any air bubbles in the chocolate, then transfer it to the refrigerator for an hour.

two Roll the modelling chocolate into a sausage and cut a piece about 1 cm (½ inch) thick. Use this to make a conical support for the rose as you shape it.

three Cut another slice of modelling chocolate, lay it on a hard surface and cover it with clingfilm. Use your thumbs to flatten the modelling chocolate and form it into the shape of a rose petal. You will need eight petals for each rose.

four Curve the first petal around the conical support.

five

seven Build up the shape of the rose, attaching petals at the bottom and overlapping them and leaving them open at the top.

six

five Curve the second petal around the opposite side of the conical support, overlapping the first petal to create a bud.

six Pinch the top edges of the petals to give them a slightly crinkled appearance.

eight Roll out some more modelling chocolate and use a rose leaf cutter to make the leaves.

nine Roll out some modelling chocolate thinly and make fans as described in Red Berry Romance (see pages 102–5).

ten Dip a fan in a little melted chocolate and attach it to the top of the cake.

eleven Trim the base of the rose and use a little more melted chocolate to attach it to the cake. Attach leaves in the same way.

eleven

ten

eight

nine

twelve Remove the cherub mould from the refrigerator and carefully loosen the edges of the mould by pulling them gently away from the chocolate. Pop the cherub very carefully out of the mould.

twelve

thirteen

thirteen Apply a little melted chocolate to the back of the cherub with a palette knife and position it on the cake. Transfer to a cake stand and decorate with berry fruits. Redcurrants look particularly nice draped over the edge of the cake stand.

1950s Glamour Cake

This sophisticated-looking cake is not that easy to make, but it does look spectacular. The delicate bows and stripes could almost be made of taffeta. It is worth having extra modelling chocolate to hand to give yourself a bit of practice rolling the strips together, as you can't reuse the modelling chocolate after it has been rolled.

Ingredients

8 cm (3 inch) round cake, 10 cm (4 inches) deep

10 cm (4 inch) round cake, 10 cm (4 inches) deep

15 cm (6 inch) round cake, 10 cm (4 inches) deep

850 g (1 lb 11 oz) white chocolate ganache (see page 28)

750 g (1½ lb) white modelling chocolate

250 g (8 oz) dark modelling chocolate

To assemble the cake

25 cm (10 inch) cake drum

8 cm (3 inch) round cake card

10 cm (4 inch) round cake card

6 dowel rods

rolling pin

ruler

small sharp knife

florists' pins

15 mm (¾ inch) wide cream ribbon

edible glue or a gluestick

one Coat the drum with white chocolate ganache (see page 30). Position the largest cake in the centre of the drum and transfer the smallest cakes to the appropriate cake cards. Use dowel rods to stack the cakes (see pages 33–4). Roll out a strip of white modelling chocolate 1.5 cm (¾ inch) thick, 11 cm (4½ inches) wide and long enough to go round the largest cake. Roll out a strip of dark modelling chocolate 1 cm (½ inch) thick, 11 cm (4½ inches) wide and to the same length as the white strip. Cut it into 11 parallel strips, each 1 cm (about ⅓ inch) wide.

two Using a little cooled boiled water to hold them in place, arrange the dark chocolate strips on the white strip, leaving a gap of 2 cm (about ¾ inch) between each strip and from each long edge.

three Carefully roll out the strip to 5 mm (¼ inch) thick, making sure that you keep the stripes as even and straight as possible.

three

one   two

four Cut the strips so that they are 10.5 cm (4¼ inches) wide and long enough to cover each tier. Don't necessarily measure from the edge, because you don't want to cut through a stripe.

four

five

five Coat the cakes with white chocolate ganache and cover the cakes with the stripes, joining them at the back with a little cooled boiled water.

six

seven

eight

nine

six Use the remaining icing to make the bows. Making sure the stripes are aligned, use the template (see page 154) to cut out a horizontal piece, 6–3 cm (2½–1¼ inches), and two vertical tails, each 2.5–11.5 cm (1–4¾ inches).

seven Fold in the end of the bow towards the centre and fold in the side towards the tip. Fold in the sides and pinch the centre.

eight Attach the central piece to the bow, wrapping it around so that the join is underneath.

nine Cut V shapes from the bottom of the tails. Curl the tails slightly, and attach them to the top edge of each strip around the cake.

ten

ten Attach the bows to the cake with melted white chocolate, holding them in place with florists' pins until they are dry. Fasten ribbon around the drum, securing the ends in place with glue. Don't forget to remove the pins before slicing the cake.

Variation Modelling chocolate is available in quite a number of colours so you could try topping a single tier version of the cake with fruit in a colour to complement the modelling chocolate of your choice. Pink chocolate and raspberries make a particularly summery display.

Bollywood

If you like bold colours or if your cake will be competing for attention with an ornate venue this is the design for you. The mixture of different shades of orange and red decorated with gold leaf makes this cake reminiscent of the most opulent of Indian palaces. Allow plenty of time for the different colours to dry at the end of each stage.

Ingredients

10 cm (4 inch) round cake , 20 cm (4 inches) deep

2 x 15 cm (6 inch) round cakes, 7 cm (3 inches) deep

20 cm (8 inch) round cake, 20 cm (4 inches) deep

25 cm (10 inch) round cake, 20 cm (4 inches) deep

2.8 kg (5 lb 10 oz) cream sugarpaste

250 g (8 oz) royal icing

tangerine, orange, poppy red and super white powder dye

gold powder

clear alcohol

To assemble the cake

30 cm (12 inch) round cake drum

35 cm (14 inch) round cake drum

10 cm (4 inch) round cake card

15 cm (6 inch) round cake card

20 cm (8 inch) round cake card

11 dowel rods

piping bag and no. 3 nozzle

2.5 cm (1 inch) paintbrush

15 mm (¾ inch) wide orange ribbon

edible glue or a gluestick

one

two

one Stack the two 15 cm (6 inch) cakes to make a
15 cm (6 inch) deep cake. Treat this as one tier. Cover the
cake drums and cakes with cream sugarpaste and stack them
(see pages 30–35). Make some orange royal icing and pipe
little balls on each tier.

two Use the same icing to pipe on the paisley pattern.
Leave to dry.

three Make pale orange royal liquid by mixing
super white and tangerine powders with a little water.
Use a large brush to cover the whole cake with a coat of
pale orange 'sponge effect'. Leave to dry.

three

four Mix a darker shade of orange by adding
more tangerine and create a stippled effect all over the
cakes. Leave to dry.

four

five

five Add a tinge of poppy red to the orange mix and repeat the operation. Leave to dry.

six Mix a little gold powder with some clear alcohol and highlight parts of the pattern on the cake. Attach a ribbon around the drum, securing the ends in position with edible glue.

six

Templates

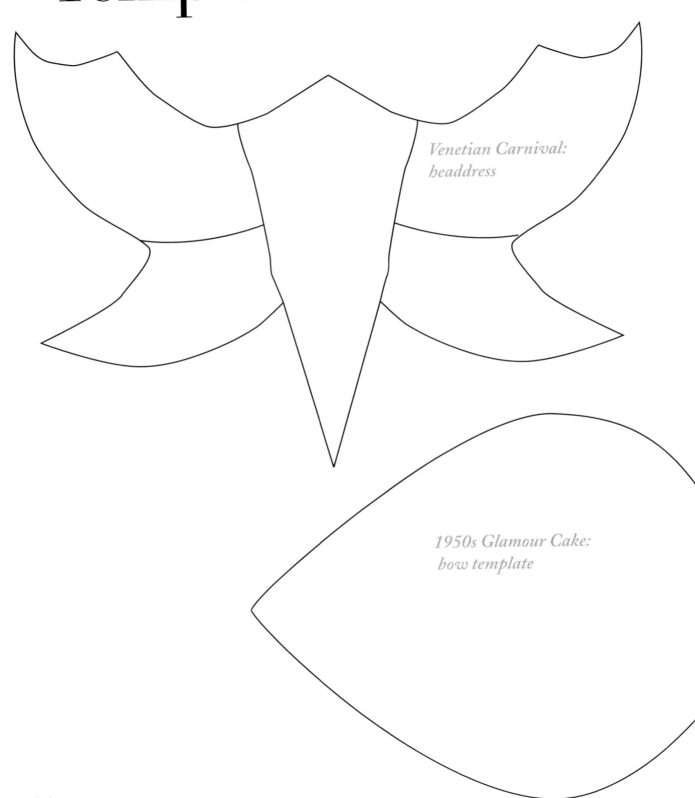

*Venetian Carnival:
headdress*

*1950s Glamour Cake:
bow template*

Venetian Carnival: mask

Glossary

Blocking a cake Polystyrene blocks provide support for tiers on a cake. Dowel rods hold the block in place and support the weight of the subsequent cake. The blocks can be covered in ribbon or obscured by decorations.

Cake drum Also known as a cake board or cake card, this supports the weight of the cake allowing it to be moved around easily. They are available in cookery shops and come in a number of shapes and sizes.

Colour dusts (lustre, petal, pearl) These can be used directly on iced cakes or decorations, or they can be added to royal icing or sugarpaste. Blending dusts with clear alcohol results in a more subtle finish.

Colour pastes Pastes are used to add vibrant colours directly to royal icing, sugarpaste and marzipan. They are available in a wide variety of colours.

Covering cakes Fruit cakes are generally covered with marzipan and then icing. Other cakes can have the icing applied directly. When calculating quantities you should take into account the extra amount required to cover the cake drum(s). (See page 31 for quantities.)

Covering drums Ensure the sugarpaste is slightly bigger in area than the cake drum. Place it over the drum and trim the edges. Cut a hole in the centre, the same size as the cake, and place the cake inside. You can disguise the join with piped decoration.

Crème pâtissière A custard that is thickened with cornflour and flavoured with vanilla. It is used in many desserts and cakes. (See recipe on page 25.)

Crystallized flowers Edible petals, flowers and fruits can be crystallized and used as cake decorations. Fresh, dry flowers and fruits are dipped in beaten egg white, then caster sugar, to create a frosted finish.

Dowel rods Thin wooden or plastic rods that are used to support pillars and tiers on cakes. They can be cut to the required length with a knife or sharp scissors.

Edible glue Available in specialist shops and used to attach decorations to cakes. It comes in a pot and should be applied with a small paintbrush. It is also available as a gluestick.

Florist's tape/florist's wire/florist's pins Can be used for a variety of applications in cake decoration from attaching decorations to creating floral displays to adorn the cake. All are available in a variety of colours.

Ganache Used as both an icing and a cake filling, ganache is made from good-quality chocolate and cream. You can buy it ready-made or make your own (see recipe page 28).

Gold leaf This delicate decoration is available as thin sheets that can be bought singly or in booklets. It is worked using tweezers and can be used directly on cakes, or to finish decorations.

Modelling chocolate Also known as cocoform, you can buy this ready-made, or you can make your own (see recipe on page 29). It can be shaped and moulded in the same way as plasticine.

Modelling tools These tools are used to create the intricate detailing for cake decorations. The curved bone tool is used for flower petals and the ball tool helps to create smooth edges. Other tools are available.

Petal paste Also known as flower paste or sugar florist's paste, this is used to make flower decorations. It has a delicate appearance as it rolls to a very thin layer. It dries hard and unused paste must be kept covered.

Pillars Pillars are used to separate the tiers of a cake. Dowel rods are inserted into the cake as the support structure and then the pillars are placed over them, with the next cake resting on top. (See page 37 for instructions.)

Piping bags and nozzles Bags come in a variety of sizes and nozzles are available in either stainless steel or plastic. There are standard sizes, as well as shaped nozzles that can be used for decorative work.

Royal icing This is traditionally made with egg whites and icing sugar (see recipe on page 23). It has a lovely glossy appearance and a pliable texture

that makes it ideal for moulding around cakes. It sets hard, however, so holds its shape well and holds decorations firmly in place.

Sugarpaste A fondant icing that is used to cover cakes and cake drums and also to create decorations. It is available in ready-to-roll packs in a variety of colours, or you can colour it yourself.

Tiered cake These are constructed using dowel rods to create a secure platform on which to rest the tiers. Each tier must have its own board the same diameter as the actual cake. (See page 34 for instructions.)

Index

Acknowledgements

This book is dedicated to Louisette and Alban, my parents.

Thank you to Jane Donovan and Jane Birch from Hamlyn for approaching me and for publishing this, my first, book. I was lucky to work with the most amazing team. Thanks to Lis Parsons for the most beautiful photography and for introducing me to Lambrini, thanks to her lovely assistant Olivia Antolik who adores cakes, but not as much as Lisa John who was always so happy to do the washing up for some kind reason and who followed us right through to the end of the book to make sure that all went smoothly. And, of course, thank you to Jo MacGregor who as well as dealing with her newborn twins had to deal with the naughtiest team in town. Guys, we had a ball in spite all the hard work and we absolutely deserved the fish and chips and vintage champagne on the last day! Thank you to Mark Stevens for doing such a stunning job on the final designs. Thank you to the Savoir Design team for being so hardworking and flexible and and for sharing my excitement about the project. To Sheena and Louise, thanks for sharing your decorating skills and secrets … what a result! Thank you to Jean and Annie who always knew that this project would happen and for helping to make it happen. Finally an apology to Bobbycat for not getting her in to any of the pictures – we did try! And 'grand merci!' to Paul for … everything.

Executive Editor Jane Donovan
Senior Editor Lisa John
Executive Art Edtior Mark Stevens
Senior Production Controller Manjit Sihra
Designer Janis Utton
All photography © Octopus Publishing Group/Lis Parsons